THE 5 CORE ABILITIES OF
HIGHLY EFFECTIVE LEADERS

THE 5 CORE ABILITIES OF HIGHLY EFFECTIVE LEADERS

ERROL LAWSON

Copyright © EWL Consultants 2016
Errol Lawson has asserted his right under the Copyright, Designs and Patents Act 1988 to be identified as the author of this work.

ISBN: 978-0-9573869-2-1

Published by EWL Consultants

errol@errollawson.com

THANK YOU

A big thank you to my wife for her encouragement,
support and patience in completing this project.

Thank you to all distinguished interview guests,
the leaders that provided the research material for this book.

Thank you to Carina Martin and Priscilla Esinam Yevu
for their writing and editing support.

A a big thank to Phil Jones, Olubisi Buraimo, Andrew Thomas
and Efrosyni Adimedes and Ian Spence for their support
and encouragement throughout the project.

The 5 Core Abilities Coaching and Mentoring Programmes

Do you want to turn your leadership team into a tribe of engaged and motivated leaders that understand your vision, are engaged, motivated and take action?

For those who want to implement the 5 core abilities method quickly and powerfully we provide one to one and group coaching for leaders and their leadership teams.

We are able to work with clients anywhere in the world. The focus of the program is to enable you to apply the best practices in this book with guidance from world-class mentors, creating a culture of high performance within your church or organisation.

Download the brochure and take the challenge at
www.the5coreabilities.com

CONTENTS

FOREWORD

I have been a leader now my whole life and in half of that time I never considered myself as one, I've always thought that leadership was only reserved for a few anointed people who came to this earth pre-packaged like a bouquet of flowers. Boy was I wrong! What a ridiculous mindset. As I began to see the influence I had on myself and the people around me, I realise that we have all been called to be a leader of some sort in different areas and unlike that pre-packaged bouquet, some of us are like a wild bush that needed to be nurtured, cultivated and pruned to fulfil our God-ordained mandate on earth. This task is an easy task to undertake and it can also be very difficult depending on what path you take. That's why The 5 Core Abilities of Highly Effective Christian Leaders and Entrepreneurs is the perfect book that allows you to cultivate simple habits that will mould each person into their own greatness.

The "The 5 Core Abilities of Highly Effective Leaders" is simple and well crafted. The bible says in **Hebrews 6:12**

> *That ye be not slothful, but be ye followers of them who through faith and patience obtained the promise*

The great mentors in this book have conquered some territories and they've done it with great results to show for it. They were not lazy in their affairs, but rather passionately navigated the unchartered waters of purpose and passion in order to be able to show themselves as real examples of great leaders. So then what excuses do we have?

Les Brown said *"Do not go where the path may lead, but rather go where there is no path and leave a trail"* I believe we all have our path to tread and by following the examples written in this book, we will emerge as leaders who not only know what to do, but DO IT! - leaders who TAKE ACTION and create powerful examples for others to follow. Maybe next time your story and wisdom will be documented in The 5 Core Abilities of Highly Effective Leaders. Remember you don't have to be great to get started, but you do have to get started in order to be great. Don't just read this book, do this book! Take the principles and apply them. I myself was refreshed and inspired as I took in some simple leadership truths. We don't need great readers, we need great LEADERS, so let go as we explore the keys to great leadership.

—**ACTION JACKSON**
YOUTH PASTOR & MOTIVATIONAL SPEAKER

When Errol asked me to write the foreword for this book I was honoured to have been asked, but also somewhat puzzled as to "why me"?

"Surely he knows better people to read and comment on this than me?" I thought to myself.

Now, having read the book I have been inspired, motivated and informed on matters ranging from leading, following, power, responsibility, giving thanks, grace, asking for help, identity and purpose. WOW!!!!

Being a "long in the tooth" professional speaker, entrepreneur and author ..., but relatively new to faith ... this book has given me the who, what, how and why of being both Christian, and a leader, both personally and professionally.

2

The five simple to follow and understand principles will help us all to step out in faith with certainty, confidence and conviction … the way we should, but too few of us actually do!

Use this book to support yourself as you grow and lead through your faith, so that we can all serve our God, our families, our communities, our churches, and ourselves in ways that God needs and wants us to do. Step out in faith, but armed with truth. Enjoy the book.

—DAVID HYNER - WWW.DAVIDHYNER.COM
PROFESSIONAL GOAL SETTING RESEARCHER AND MOTIVATIONAL SPEAKER

It all started so well - vision, enthusiasm, passion, dedication. You put in all the effort you could and all the hours possible, yet still it all fell apart and you were left burnt out. Have you ever been in this position? All your best endeavours producing some results but taking all the energy you can find and pushing you well beyond your reserves. If you have ever been in this position you will know how draining, devastating and long lasting the effects can be. Trying to accomplish everything alone is not profitable in the long run.

I have had the benefit of being a people manager and leader in business, ministry and the corporate world for the last 15 years. In this time I have witnessed burnout countless times, and personally experienced it on many occasions. There is a generation rising that cannot afford the setbacks this brings. They have the zeal, enthusiasm and grounding in the things of God to be agents of change and make an undeniable impact in the lives of others. This is why "The 5 Core Abilities of Highly Effective Leaders" is such a timely book.

This is a book that every leader in church, business or the community needs to read and should revisit periodically. It teaches how to successfully communicate the vision you have whilst exhibiting the true characteristics of a leader. This then allows you to be a key person of influence, one that attracts the right team members to you - vision carriers, vision birthers and vision sustainers.

Errol has succinctly captured the 5 keys that will unlock your leadership potential and take you to the next level. These 5 keys are packed with revolutionary tools and messages touching on church growth, culture, building an empowered team and the need for humility and above all prayer. I have certainly drawn from these tools and will be passing them on to my teams.

In the relatively short time I have known Errol (2 years and counting), I have seen him lead in ministry, the marketplace and the home. He leads with his teams in mind and on his heart and truly lives to the characteristics of which he writes. A godly man first and foremost, he does all things to the glory of God. Errol has made an impact locally in the United Kingdom and also internationally. He is a known and well-respected author, speaker, leadership coach and trainer. It is a privilege to labour with him in the Lord.

Enjoy this book and be blessed.

—**REVEREND CATHERINE LABINJO**
MINISTER, NEW FAITH GENERATION CHURCH
AWARD-WINNING SPEAKER, LEADERSHIP COACH AND ENTREPRENEUR

ABOUT THE AUTHOR

WHAT OTHERS ARE SAYING

"Errol delivered a highly engaging and very powerful session to UpRising's Fastlaners participants. His honest and open approach helped a group of unemployed young people to draw on their personal experience to understand their skills and realise their ability to succeed. Building resilience and motivation isn't an easy task, but Errol's workshop really did just that and inspired participants to strive for the best and believe in their own self worth. I thoroughly recommended working with Errol and look forward to doing so again soon – thank you!"

—LOUISE BELSOM
SENIOR PROJECT MANAGER AT UPRISING LEADERSHIP

"Probably the best coach I've ever had."

—HEATHER ROBERTS,
EXECUTIVE HEADTEACHER, EQUITAS ACADMIES TRUST

"Errol delivered a workshop of 'telling your story' with some disadvantaged young people in a programme I was organising. His input was perfect and hugely impactful. We provided Errol with a fairly broad brief around motivation and team building, and he was able to take this and tailor the perfect input for the group. They left motivated, more connected than they had ever been, and really fired up for their future. It was exactly what we as an organisation wanted, and importantly the young people took so much from it. A joy to work with, and cannot wait to find ways to connect Errol with our programme again".

—RYS FARTHING
DIRECTOR OF STRATEGY AND IMPACT UP: UNLOCKING POTENTIAL

I started out 20 years ago coaching teenagers, and currently our company works with between 30,000 and 50,000 young people each year, from the high achievers to those from some of the toughest and hardest to reach backgrounds, in prisons and in more than 100 schools all across the UK. Find out more about our schools work at www.emerge-leadership.com.

What makes my coaching transformational is that I personally went from being homeless at 16 years old and being involved with tough street gangs to turning it around and becoming an award winning entrepreneur, author and a pastor in my local church. So, I know what it's like to feel stuck in life and without clear purpose or direction but very importantly I also know what it takes to get back up out of a seemingly impossible situation, start walking with The Lord and see things completely turn around.

I started my first enterprise at 19 years old, running events and concerts in the local community. Now as City Leader for a Global Business coaching and training company, DENT Global, I have the opportunity to coach some of the most amazing entrepreneurs from around the world, helping them to build great businesses and solve some of the world's greatest problems. Find out more at www.dent.global

What's helped me to become successful at coaching entrepreneurs and leaders is the fact that many of the same principles and skills that I have used to get results coaching tough young people, are totally transferable when working with business leaders, senior managers, start up entrepreneurs, elite entre-preneurs, you name it.

Every leader or business owner that I get to work with gets results in their lives.

✝ They get a clear understanding of what their 'why' is.

✝ They regularly have those 'aha' moments that result in financial gains, improved performance and healthier relationships.

✝ They discover the confidence needed to be able to confront difficult situations and step into their biggest challenges.

✝ They get clarity about their mission and vision and their personal values.

✝ They overcome the procrastination trap and start writing and publishing the books and blogs that they always wanted to do.

✝ They start to build their brand and build an online profile that positions them to be an influential leader in their industry.

✝ They discover who their ideal clients are and they create and sell products/service to them.

✝ They take action on their goals and start getting paid doing what they love.

The 5 Core Abilities Coaching and Mentoring Programmes

For those who want to implement the 5 Core Abilities Method quickly and powerfully we provide one to one and group coaching for leaders and their leadership teams.

We are able to work with clients anywhere in the world. The focus of the program is to enable you to apply the best practices in this book with guidance from world-class mentors, creating a culture of high performance within your church or organisation.

Download the brochure and take the challenge at
www.the5coreabilities.com

Other books by Errol Lawson

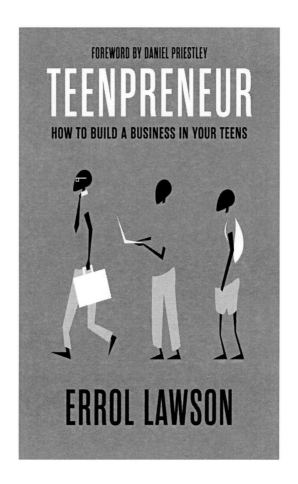

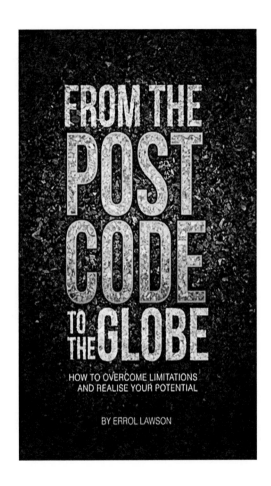

Available on *www.amazon.com*

BACKGROUND

LOTS OF LEADERS, NOT ENOUGH LEADERSHIP

Imagine a world in which every church goer was executing their purpose and doing exactly what they where called to do in the places that they were called to be. In the last few centuries Christian men and women have been at the forefront of social change and innovation around the world. In education, health care, science, youth work, social reform, Christians have been inspired by heir faith to step out and make a big difference in the world. For most people the concept of becoming a significant leader is a daunting task. Where do you start? How do you do it? Am I good enough? Which path do I take? Do I need to get a mentor or not? and so on. My goal is to help you to get the clarity you need to be able to grow as a leader in your business or in your personal or professional life and become all that you were designed to be.

THE RESEARCH

106 influential Christian leaders from the UK, Africa, America and Australia from the fields of business, academia and church based ministry were interviewed and asked a variety of questions about their leadership experiences. The primary criteria for the selection of those that were interviewed was that they have made an international impact with their work. Meaning that they were not just leading people or proj-ects on a local basis, but there was clear evidence they were making an impact in different countries around the world. (You can listen to all of the interviews by going to *www.errollawson.com/podcast*)

Each of the leaders interviewed demonstrate to us that it is possible for someone with a dream or goal in their heart, to not just fulfill that goal but to excel in it, and in the pursuit of that dream to become a leader of significance. Someone that people admire. Someone that has influence and someone that people look up to and respect.

You can be born with leadership skills and ability but the evidence showed that you become a true leader 'on the way' ... that is *In pursuit of your purpose or goal.* You have to get out and do something!

My discovery whilst interviewing these leaders, was that very few of them set out to be a significant leader. However all of them have amazing stories of how they set out to make a SIGNIFICANT IMPACT. They became leaders along the way. As a bi product. None of them were out to play small. They wanted to make a BIG difference. If you are wanting to make a big difference with your life, and solve meaningful problems this is the book for you.

The Mission:

I am passionate about coaching and developing leaders and it's something I have done for 20 years. Which is why I have written this book. To equip and empower the body of Christ to fulfil their leadership potential. Why? Because just like my mentor John Maxwell says "Everything rises and falls on leadership". Our businesses, our churches, or our homes, all depend on having great leadership. Great leadership doesn't just happen, it develops daily. This book gives you the opportunity to learn from some of the best.

All of the leaders interviewed were Christians. You will notice a lot of references to the Christian faith throughout my book. I've been a pastor in a local church for 10 years now, so quite naturally you will hear some of my faith perspectives coming through as you read. My faith is my bedrock.

The Framework:

Their are lots of abilities that great leaders have or need to develop and there are many great books written on leadership. From my research I seek to offer a different perspective. With my team, I have gone through all of the interviews, considered all of the challenges the leaders faced along their journeys and how they were able to overcome them and attain success. The leaders all demonstrated a myriad of abilities and as challenging as it was **we were able to categorise the abilities into** 5 core abilities. 5 abilities that I believe are essential to leadership success in the ever changing times that we live in. In this book I teach you how to develop the 5 abilities and to grow yourself as a leader. I encourage you to not only learn them but to lead others to them and empower others to step into their biggest challenges.

The 5 core abilities are:

1 The ability to create and communicate a compelling vision

These leaders mastered the art of being able to create and communicate a compelling vision. One that motivated people to take action. One that inspired others to follow.

2 The ability to create and manage wealth

The ability to manage both personal and organisational funds is crucial. The two are intrinsically linked. Learning how to raise funds for your vision is also key.

3 The ability to defy self-doubt and lead with conviction

The ability to overcome, fear, setbacks, rejection, the imposter syndrome and to continue to move forward in the face of adversity.

4   **The ability to focus on the essentials and eliminate or delegate the rest**

Knowing your strengths and being able to delegate your weaknesses. Getting out of the way and letting go of some things so that the people with the necessary skills can step in. Many leaders confessed they learned this the hard way.

5   **The ability to get the best out of the people you lead - whether they like you or not**

What do you do when the people you lead let you down? They reject you, turn their backs on you, don't show up, underperform? Somehow you still need to maintain a level headed humility, engage your team, inspire them, rise above the circumstances and achieve the desired outcomes. A tough skill but these leaders were able to do just that.

Enjoy the journey.

The 5 Core Abilities Coaching and Mentoring Programmes

Do you want to turn your leadership team into a tribe of engaged and motivated leaders that understand your vision, are engaged, motivated and take action?

For those who want to implement the 5 core abilities method quickly and powerfully we provide one to one and group coaching for leaders and their leadership teams.

We are able to work with clients anywhere in the world. The focus of the program is to enable you to apply the best practices in this book with guidance from world-class mentors, creating a culture of high performance within your church or organisation.

Download the brochure and take the challenge at
www.the5coreabilities.com

The ability to
create and communicate
a compelling vision

Chapter 1

DISCOVERING THE VISION
FOR YOUR LIFE, BUSINESS
OR MINISTRY

Every leader wants a mission statement: a powerful sense of purpose that inspires us, guides us, and thoroughly permeates every area of our lives. What is the difference between us deciding on a personal vision for our lives versus receiving a vision from God for our lives?

But this kind of compelling, life-altering vision isn't something that we can create on our own. We need the continual inspiration and input of God to make envisioned dreams a reality. Think of your vision not simply as a "mission statement" that you create, but as a priceless treasure that is bestowed on you by God. When you get a vision from God for your life it will be greater than anything you can imagine.

How can you determine that your vision is truly coming from the Lord? How do you know that the prompting you feel is heavenly rather than worldly? These are tough questions, and they don't have easy answers. I spoke to Marisa Shadrick, an internationally renowned Christian author and speaker, in order to get her perspective on this issue.

Marisa describes herself as an "encourager at heart," and says that her ultimate goal is to strengthen the Body of Christ through her ministerial work. Her heart's deepest desire is to help other people overcome their pain and transform fears into faith.

Without question, your ability to grab hold of a 'God sized' vision for your life, business or ministry is going change everything. In this chapter, we'll be examining each of the characteristics that set God's calling or vision apart from our own personal desires.

CHARACTERISTIC #1: IT STANDS OUT

To truly understand the nature and genesis of vision, we need to look to the examples provided for us in the Bible. This is the best way to determine whether a call is truly from the Lord or just our own desires masquerading as His will.

Some of the Kingdom's most influential visionaries received their call through supernatural means. Many great men and women heard God's voice directly, as we can read in the stories of Moses and Isaiah. Still more great leaders discovered God's vision through dreams or other phenomena. Think of Joseph, who learned of God's plan to make him ruler of Egypt through cryptic dreams, or of the prophet Ezekiel, who dreamed of an angel feeding him the scroll of God's word. Despite what skeptics may tell you, God is still visibly active in the world. He still uses these kinds of supernatural interventions to get our attention—we just need to look out for them!

Too often, however, leaders become discouraged because God hasn't given them an explicit sign. Calls to service aren't always that dramatic. God communicates with each of us in a totally unique way, because He alone knows how we were made. He may speak powerfully to you through study of His word, or appreciation of the incredible world He has created. He may show you His will in the prayers of a mentor or the lyrics of your favourite worship song. So pay attention to the thou-sands of opportunities you have to hear from God each day. Pursue fellowship with other strong believers. Spend time in nature. Dedicate yourself to prayer, worship, and periodic fasting. The book of Job in the Old Testament says it best:

For God does speak—now one way,
now another—though no one perceives it.

—Job 3:3, NIV

Marisa Shadrick was one of those people who *does* perceive God's word in her life. During our conversation, she told me that she clearly recognised God's initial call on her life. "God was calling me to a different form of ministry," she said, "outside of a traditional sense. He was calling me to write. That seemed very foreign to me, but I thought, 'If this is something God wants me to do, then I need to look into it.'"

Marisa particularly remembers attending a Christian writer's conference while she was still very unsure about her calling. During a powerful prayer session, a woman called aspiring writers up on stage to receive a blessing.

"I went up, and there were so many people!" Marisa recalled. "This woman who was praying for people reached through the crowd, grabbed my wrist, and pulled me through the crowd. She looked at me and said, 'You are a scribe for the Lord.' At that moment, I said, 'Okay God—I get it!'" That extraordinary experience confirmed that the call she was feeling really was from the Lord. Perhaps you've experienced the same kind of spiritual experience or have felt a pull in a certain direction every time you read scripture or pray. That's usually a good indication that the call you're feeling is truly from the Lord.

"God does it in different ways," Marisa said. "Sometimes it's through His word, and sometimes it's through a prophetic word, but He confirms what He's doing in your heart."

CHARACTERISTIC #2: *IT MAKES YOU UNCOMFORTABLE*

We also need to make sure that we don't modify God's call to fit our own desires or comfort levels. People frequently make the mistake of thinking that God must be calling them to tasks that they are already good at. Perhaps you've been feeling a call toward ministering overseas or starting a new business, but are resisting it because you don't have the right skill set now.

Here's the thing that we, as Christian leaders, need to remember: God rarely wants us to stay in our comfort zone! We are the continuation of a long leadership tradition that includes evangelists like the apostle Paul, activists like Dr. Martin Luther King, Jr., and missionaries like Mother Theresa. All these people were pulled from their daily existence—sometimes suddenly or even violently—and placed on an entirely new course of service. If your call is truly from God, it will entail some sacrifices and personal growth.

Why does God call us outside our comfort zone? Often, it's so that we can learn to depend on His guidance. According to Marisa, God often asks us for two things: sacrifice and surrender. "As soon as I started taking it seriously and realising that this was what God was calling me to do," Marisa shared, "I did have to step down from some of the formal ministries I was involved in." Are there things that this calling will require you to give up or put aside for a time?

God's call can also challenge us by demanding that we surrender our talents to Him. People frequently make the mistake of thinking that God must be calling them to do what they are already good at. That's because we have a lot of pride in the things that we do well— but it's a pride that can seriously impede our ability to carry out God's will. Marisa knows this fact well. "I have the gift of administration," she told me. "So I want to organise God! We need to bring some of those things to the foot of the Cross, come to the Lord and ask what He would have me do next. That's where the passion comes from. We begin to fall in love with God, and the Scriptures come to life, and our mind is renewed and we begin to realise where our place is." If we are focused on our own abilities and talents, then we can't allow God to work through us.

In the end, this surrender and sacrifice gives us perspective. It helps us thrive in our roles as tools in God's loving hands. "It's not me, it's God doing things through me," Marisa said. "Everything I'm doing is so out of my comfort zone that I need to depend on Him for everything."

CHARACTERISTIC #3: IT DOESN'T LET YOU STAND STILL

God also wants us to grow and better ourselves, a process that can only occur if He asks us for things we aren't yet totally prepared to give. After all, your calling is a way for God to work in your life as well as the lives around you. He wants to see you grow as you change the world! So a calling from God will necessarily entail personal growth.

Once she had decided to dedicate herself to her new calling, Marisa committed to learning as much as she could about the craft of writing. She attended more writers' conferences, studied the publishing industry in depth, and honed her composition skills. Then she put in the strenuous work of building up a readership platform and marketing herself to the world.

"When I started writing, it was comfortable and safe," Marisa said. "And then all of a sudden I realised: writers are speakers, and speakers are writers. It's a marriage that goes hand-in-hand. The speaking part was something I definitely wasn't prepared for." But instead of giving in to her inhibitions, Marisa joined a public speaking organisation to hone her skills. Every meeting tested her resolve, but God kept telling her to go back. She recalls an episode where her mind was stretched.

"I was doing a speech, waiting outside in a patio because it wasn't time yet to go on," she said. "And God said to me, 'What would you say if you could speak to the nations?' And I thought that was a loaded question—I had no idea! Why would that even come up?" As it turns out, the organisation Marisa was a part of hosts an international public speaking competition every year. She began to feel that God was prompting her to compete and use the publicity to share His word.

To her own surprise, Marisa went on to win at the local and regional level. Only a year after beginning her public speaking journey, she was ranked among the hundred best speakers in the world—and she was able to use that new platform to grow her ministry. From that point on, Marisa made some resolutions. "I told God, 'No matter what You say, no matter if it sounds huge or far- fetched, I'm going to take you at Your word. I'm not going to question it!' If God is speaking something to you, and you're wondering how this could come to pass, then just take the next step. Just trust Him. He will open those doors."

Of course, not everyone experiences those kinds of rapid results. Even Marisa admitted that she was shocked to see such a huge response to her work. It can take years to see your vision completely—or even partially—fulfilled. But you will never get anywhere if you aren't willing to put in hard work over a long period of time. If Marisa had allowed her fear and self-doubt to cloud her vision, she would never have built the thriving ministry she administrates today. And she recognises that her growth happened one step at a time, and was always directed by the Lord.

"We don't always see the macro view, the big picture," she said. "All we have is today. Sometimes that can be challenging because we would love to see the big picture—but do we really want to? If God had told me that I would be speaking, "You're going to have an online profile where people all over the world will be able to see who you are", I would have said "No way!" But he grew me into those large shoes. It was step by step.

A true God-given vision will never allow you to settle for anything less than your best. It inspires you to take the next step, and the next step, and the next step, until you have reached heights you never could have envisioned before! If you're willing to put the time and effort into making yourself better, then you will reap the rewards that come from passion-ate dedication.

To recap, here are a few of the characteristics of Godly vision that we've described in this chapter:

✝ A Godly vision makes an undeniable impact on your life, whether through a supernatural experience or a consistent prompting
✝ A Godly vision pushes you outside your comfort zone and challenges your status quo
✝ A Godly vision inspires you to be better and keep pressing toward your goal

Chapter 2

COMMUNICATING THE VISION EFFECTIVELY

So you've got an awesome vision—congratulations! Here's the part where things can get very confusing, very fast. Now you need to figure out how to communicate that vision in a **compelling way** to others so that you can build a solid support system or customer base. This is sadly where many leaders' plans tend to fall apart: they aren't sure how to spread the word without feeling pushy. **They** shy away from publicity because they are not familiar with basic advertising principles. We may explain our vision, but we may not know how to market it effectively.

Enter Dan Maudhub, a long-time pioneer in the world of advertising. After starting a brand-consulting firm at the age of 24, Dan developed a passion for marketing. He heads the digital creative marketing agency, Wonderful Creative, where he helps brands and businesses all over the world to refine their message. As a pastor and administrator at Jubilee Church, Dan is also very passionate about helping ministry leaders real-ise their full, God-given potential. He is fascinated by the relationship between what we do at church and what we do at work.

With the benefit of his many years of experience, Dan is highly knowl-edgeable about the principles of marketing. You may assume that these strategies only apply to high-powered businesses, but it's just the opposite: every business and organisation, no matter how small, can benefit from good marketing. It's the best way to move a vision out of your heart and into the hearts of others.

I hope that some of Dan's marketing advice will help you spread your vision to a wider audience!

PRINCIPLE #1: BUILD YOUR CORE

Your strong, God-given vision is an incredible asset. But without some guidance, it can develop into a weakness as well. Many leaders, proud of their expansive visions, become overconfident and assume that they can do no wrong. That can lead to big problems down the line. So how can we avoid running into this problem in our own leadership journeys? Dan insists that the key is to surround yourself with accountability partners.

"I'm a very visionary leader," Dan said. "I love new things! So I've had to work on not just being led by vision, but making sure there is a clear vision and that the timing is right. You could have a great idea and plan, but do it at the wrong time and it fails. My biggest weakness is shooting ahead too quickly. So I've learned to take a step back, engage with people, and get them on board too." In finding that core of trusted partners, make sure that you choose people with honesty and integrity. As we can read in Proverbs:

Wounds from a friend can be trusted.

—Proverbs 27:6

What a counterintuitive statement! But it's completely true: we all need correction from time to time. Since the beginning of his career, Dan has always surrounded himself with mentors who can offer both spiritual and business advice when he needs it. "You've got to put good, like-minded people around you," he said. But "like-minded" doesn't mean that those people always agree with you. "In my leadership journey," Dan said, "I've always had people around me who could speak into my life. I've always had mentors, people who have helped to train and equip me. For me, being accountable has been a key part of my journey. I make sure that I can bounce things off people who aren't just 'yes men', but who will ask me the tough questions."

Here is a list of practical ways that you can encourage healthy honesty in your business or organisation's "core" group:

☩ Respectfully ask everyone on the team to contribute opinions and ideas

☩ Encourage discussion of ideas and try to get multiple perspectives

☩ Don't shoot people down just because they disagree with you

☩ Actually *implement* the suggestions that you get from others, rather than just listening to them

This kind of approach reaps great rewards on an institutional level. "I always say that a church is only as strong as its core group of people," Dan said. "That's the people who give input, who take responsibility and ownership. If you can get people mobilised and engaged, you can do a lot more." Many people working together can craft a more compelling, conscientious, and nuanced message than one person slaving away on their own. Think of ways that you can engage others to be part of your core team.

27

PRINCIPLE #2: *KNOW YOURSELF*

Now that you have a strong core of people to keep you on course, it's important that everyone is aware of your message. "Be clear on who you are," Dan advised. "All good marketing starts with a very clear message. Know what makes you, you! God's created us to have different expressions of the Kingdom: it's all about knowing what you can bring to that equation." If not everyone understands and embraces your vision, then you will never work as an effective team.

Spend focused time with your core team discussing your organisation's identity. Ask these kinds of questions of the group:

☩ What are our ultimate goals? If money and time were no object, what would we like to see accomplished in the world?

☩ If we had to describe our organisation's mission in three words, what would they be?

☩ What makes us different from other businesses/ministries out there now?

A vision is a bit like a bucket full of holes. No matter how compelling or powerful it may be, it will always leak—unless you constantly pour time and energy back into it. "Are you clear on your values and DNA?" Dan asks his clients. It's always better to focus on doing a few things well than to spread yourself thin trying to "do it all." Look at your team and your passions. Figure out what you do better than anyone else. Then, make sure everyone knows about it! "Develop strategies that build from there," Dan advised. "So many times, in both business and ministry, people just *do stuff*. They run programs and campaigns without being sure why they're doing it! That's why I always take leaders back and say, 'Why should we do this?' That's what breeds passion and success."

As a leader, it is your responsibility to create a culture in which everyone fully understands your vision, feels responsible for its success, and has the passion to share it with the rest of the world. Even during tough times, the businesses that don't scrimp on marketing budgets are the ones who continue to pull in profit. Likewise, the churches that consis-tently share their vision with the community are the ones who make a lasting impact.

PRINCIPLE #3: ADAPT YOUR MESSAGE

If Jesus were alive today, would He use Twitter? Dan certainly thinks so! "I always say that Jesus was the best communicator who ever lived," he said. "He took a completely new proposition to the world: the Kingdom of God! He reunited people to their Father, he opened the way for a new life and a whole new faith. He just told it in simple stories that the average person could understand. He didn't use big words or phrases: He brought it down to where the people were."

One of Jesus' biggest strengths was that He adapted His message to suit His audience. If He was speaking in front of a crowd of ordinary people, He often used dramatic stories to get His point across. When He was talking to the religious leaders in the Temple, He used intelli-gent arguments and examples from the Hebrew Scriptures. In intimate discussions with His disciples, He spoke frankly about the challenges of following God. Of course, the fundamentals of His message always stayed the same. Jesus merely adapted the form based on context. And He kept repeating Himself, over and over. Sometimes it even made Him frustrated to say the same things over and over.

The same principle applies to us today: sharing your message one time just isn't going to cut it! There are a huge number of distractions vying for people's attention in our busy modern times. To get their attention, you need to be consistent and innovative in your communication, exploring a range of different ways to get your message across.

Everyone processes information in a different way. Some people are aurally focused, learning best by listening. Some people process information visually, through videos and presentations. Still others find it easiest to participate in activities or to read. Storytelling is another extremely powerful tool that many leaders forget to use. A great story draws people in and holds their interest, without feeling like an advertisement. Maybe your message could best be shared by an engaging narrative-based video or blog post. Experiment with different ways of explaining your organisation's journey, and then write the story you would want to read. Think about the ways that you have overcome obstacles, persevered through hard times, or come up with a clever solution to a problem. All of these make for fantastic, uplifting story opportunities—so be on the lookout!

Perhaps you can experiment with recording promotional videos, writing interesting blog posts, or just working to make your website more attractive to people who want to find more about your vision. "If someone comes onto your website," Dan asks his clients, "are they going to understand what you're all about? Do they get your ethos, your personality? Websites have become the window through which people see the world."

Dan gave me a list of some of his favourite ways to reach out to the community. Here they are:

✝ Social media (Facebook, Twitter, and beyond)—These "new media" are fantastic tools for engaging younger audiences.

✝ Community events—Holding a fun event is one of the easiest ways to increase your visibility and grow a steady base of clients or supporters.

✝ Podcasts—A fantastic resource if you're looking to reach professionals on the go.

✝ Company or ministry blogs—These are a great way to give in-depth background on your mission and plans.

✝ Word of mouth—If you can get people excited, they will pass that excitement on to others. This is one of the most powerful kinds of marketing.

New technologies present a host of exciting ways to reach out to potential customers or ministry partners. "Are you engaged on social media, showing the fun stuff you're doing and the vibe that is going on?" Dan always asks his clients. He believes strongly in exploring many different kinds of media to reach people in the community. As he said: "You've got an easy way of communicating what God is doing to the community." So use it!

PRINCIPLE #4: MIX IT UP

"Be able to test it," Dan said. "Try things and see how they go. Be able to measure things." Large corporations understand how this concept works: they make it a habit to frequently gather feedback on their projects and products. "One of the things you see a lot in business is that people will run a campaign, measure the results, and then make it better," Dan said. This strategy ensures that the company is constantly aware of and solving problems.

Unfortunately, we don't always apply this kind of procedure in our ministries and small businesses. "We continue to do the same old thing, time in and time out!" Dan said. "We don't change things up, or think about things creatively." Much of this hesitation comes from fear. We're afraid of putting ourselves out there more prominently because our new strategy might not work. But in doing that, we hamper our own ability to branch out and set ourselves apart from our competitors. "It comes down to trust," Dan said. "It's being able to trust that God and His promises are bigger than your fear of failure. The more I've applied that to my life, the more amazing things I've seen."

As a recap, here are some of the strategies that we've seen for sharing your vision with others:

✟ Gather a "core team" of competent, honest people to help you on your way

✟ Define the characteristics and mission statements that set you apart from other organisations

✟ Put your message in front of your audience consistently

✟ Adjust the form of your message depending on the audience you're trying to reach

✟ Experiment with new, different kinds of media in order to attract more interest

✟ Don't be afraid to take risks

Chapter 3 | RECOVERING WHEN YOU HAVE LOST YOUR WAY

Maybe you know that God has given you a powerful vision, but aren't sure how to manifest it in a business or ministry. Maybe an unrelated personal circumstance has interfered with your passion for your work. Maybe you're trying to communicate your vision to others, but no one else seems to "get it." Maybe you're even starting to worry that you've chosen the wrong path. The last thing you want to do is lose your pas-sion, but you're not sure how to move forward.

Thankfully, you're not alone. Every single effective leader has struggled, at some point, with these kinds of doubts. Known affectionately as "Lady J" by many of her friends and clients, Dr. Jovannah Ellison is a successful business coach and speaker who spends her life building up others. She's passionate about helping others find "the song inside of themselves."

As the leader of Maximum Potential Academy, "Lady J" has spent many years formally and informally coaching other entrepreneurs. She equips others with confidence and clarity, and makes it her personal mission to send out business leaders who are prepared to share their vision with the world. She is also a pastor's wife at the Church of God in Christ, which has two campuses in Birmingham and Montgomery, Alabama—another role that has taught her how to encourage and strengthen others.

I hope that her wise words will help you to understand how to deal with these kinds of difficult questions when they arrive. We'll also be looking at lessons from the life of the Biblical prophet Elijah, one of the most powerful leaders of the Old Testament, who also grappled with feelings of doubt throughout his entire ministry.

PRINCIPLE #1: "US-FOCUSED" INTO "THEM-FOCUSED"

According to Dr. Ellison, the absolute best thing you can do when you're feeling stuck and uninspired is to rededicate yourself to serving others. She believes that over time, we become too focused on our own insecurities and lose sight of the love that should be our primary motivation. "Eight years ago I moved from a little city called Los Angeles to Montgomery, Alabama," she shared. "Big shift! It was a huge transition, and my prayer became: 'Lord, help me blossom where I'm planted.' In helping me, the Lord showed me to serve outwardly. Put the focus on other people. Instead of just looking at what you're going through, or what's wrong in your own world, think about how you can empower others."

Sometimes we need to "think small" for a time in order to rediscover our purpose. Stop thinking just about the big picture and think instead about the tangible, everyday ways you can help others. "When people think they don't have anything to offer the world, that's rooted in selfishness," she said. "We're always thinking 'Who will listen to *me*?' or '*I'm* so stuck.' We're so us-focused! Being others-focused will help get us moving again." Actions as seemingly small-scale as volunteering at a local homeless shelter or writing a letter to a friend who is going through a difficult time can work wonders for your passion.

Much of the Prophet Elijah's ministry was also structured around helping others. He spent time with people who were hurting, learned about their needs, and used his position as a prophet to help them. In the book of 1 Kings, we can read about a famous incident when Elijah performed a miracle for a starving widow:

> Elijah said to her, "Don't be afraid. Go home and do as you have said. But first make a small loaf of bread for me from what you have and bring it to me, and then make something for yourself and your son. For this is what the LORD, the God of Israel, says: 'The jar of flour will not be used up and the jug of oil will not run dry until the day the Lord sends rain on the land.' She went away and did as Elijah had told her. So there was food every day for Elijah and for the woman and her family.

> —1 KINGS 7:13-15

This wasn't the only way that Elijah served others. Raising children from the dead, bringing rain and healing back to the land—he was constantly using his position as an anointed prophet and leader to bring hope and healing to the lives of others. God often gave him these tasks during times of depression or disillusionment, helping the prophet to refocus on the ultimate goal of serving others.

If you're feeling as if you've lost your sense of vision and purpose, then maybe it's time for you to get back to every Christian's most important mandate: loving others as you love yourself. Dr. Ellison employs this powerful maxim: "Give to somebody else what you wish you had for yourself." By pouring ourselves into others, we often find that we are renewed ourselves.

PRINCIPLE #2: *NEGATIVITY INTO POSITIVITY*

Sometimes, we lose sight of our vision because we have been stuck in negative thought patterns for too long. Because of setbacks or long periods of stagnation, we start to feel that we aren't adequate to carry out the dreams that God has given us. As anyone who's experienced this can attest, it can be so difficult to break the bondage of discouraging thoughts.

"I've been there! I understand what it's like to be stuck, to feel like you're in a place you'll never get out of," Dr. Ellison said. "When you're stuck, you need to change the way you ask yourself questions. Instead of saying 'Why me?' or 'I don't have enough money or time,' or 'My family doesn't believe in me,' reframe the way you talk to yourself. Ask yourself this question: 'What does this make possible?'"

Changing your mentality is an incredibly important step toward rediscovering your passion. It may sound cliché, but "looking on the bright side" can really help you to remember why you embraced your vision in the first place. Not experiencing the fast growth you would like to see in your business? Perhaps you have more time to spend learning from your mentors, or building quality relationships with potential clients. Not feeling the same drive for your ministry that you used to? Maybe you now have more energy to dedicate to studying God's word and learning about His will for your future.

In addition to the ever-important "What does this make possible?" question, Dr. Ellison also uses some of these additional mental exercises to stimulate positive ideas:

✝ What are people asking me for? What kind of advice do people come to me to receive?

✝ How can I create something that will serve even more people?

✝ What are some of the needs I see around me?

✝ What makes my heart sing? What makes me come alive?

Ask these questions not just of yourself, but of some of the people around you. Be bold! Get feedback from your spouse, your employees, your friends, and your bosses. If people say that you're a great encourager, then think about the ways that you can build up the hurting people in your life. If you're passionate about a fine art like carpentry or painting, then film a few videos of yourself and start a teaching channel online. If others tell you that you're a fantastic cook, then look into that and make use of it.

Asking yourself about new possibilities and getting specific feedback about your strengths can help revitalise you and fill you with a new zeal for your vision.

PRINCIPLE #3: *PAIN INTO PURPOSE*

What do you do when the obstacle to your vision isn't just insecurity or discouragement, but heartbreak? For Dr. Ellison, Christmas time has always been a time of painful memories. "My dad left our family on

Christmas Eve," she said. "I was just seven years old, and a seven year old doesn't understand why Daddy has to leave on Christmas Eve, of all days. I pleaded, 'Please don't go,' but no matter how much begging I did, he walked away. I grew up with bitterness and unforgiveness. I was raised in a loving home by a mom who has always taught us to love and forgive. I just wasn't ready."

But as she grew older and was convicted to coach others, Dr. Ellison realised that this bitterness was hampering her vision. As she said: "I had to take the first step and forgive my dad." So Dr. Ellison surprised her father at his seventieth birthday party. He embraced her, and together they began to rebuild their relationship. "I gave myself permission to open that door again and dislodge the root of bitterness, so that I could coach more effectively," Dr. Ellison said. "In turn, that has brought so many people on board whose fathers or spouses have also left. They ask me, 'How can I use my pain for a purpose?'"

Over the years, that phrase—"using pain for a purpose"—has become one of Dr. Ellison's favourite encouragements. This can be incredibly demanding task, but tragedy and pain are inevitable parts of life. As leaders, we need to find ways to push through discouragement and doubt, and keep doing what we're called to do even in the midst of turmoil. One of the best ways to do that is to use that pain to inspire others. Somewhere out there is a person who is dealing with exactly the problems you've dealt with. Whether your setback is the death of a loved one, a period of depression, or a difficult illness, you can find someone who has gone through the same.

Hunted and abused, Elijah was certainly no stranger to painful experiences. In fact, at one point in his story, he was so depressed and purposeless that he actually asked God to end his life:

> *Elijah was afraid and ran for his life. When he came to Beersheba in Judah, he left his servant there while he himself went a day's journey into the wilderness. He came to a broom bush, sat down under it and prayed that he might die. 'I have had enough, Lord,' he said. 'Take my life; I am no better than my ancestors.*

—1 KINGS 19: 3-4, NIV

It's an incredibly relatable for anyone who has experienced grief: the solitude, the doubt, and the despair. But God answered Elijah in a very unusual and powerful fashion:

> *Then a great and powerful wind tore the mountains apart and shattered the rocks before the Lord, but the Lord was not in the wind. After the wind there was an earthquake, but the Lord was not in the earthquake. After the earthquake came a fire, but the Lord was not in the fire. And after the fire came a gentle whisper. When Elijah heard it, he pulled his cloak over his face and went out and stood at the mouth of the cave. Then a voice said to him, "What are you doing here, Elijah?"*

Over and over again, God asks Elijah that same question: "What are you doing here?" God encouraged the prophet to look past the pain into a new purpose. Elijah had forgotten another of Dr. Ellison's favourite sayings: "When you lose your why, you lose your way." He had allowed his vision to be overshadowed by the fears and discouragements he saw around him. But God changed that by drawing Elijah's focus away from everything that was going wrong, toward Himself.

Dr. Ellison agreed that hearing directly from God is the only way to experience true spiritual rejuvenation. "Everything needs to be based in prayer," she said. "Ask God to help you process this pain first. You will become more effective if you heal first. As you're in that process, it doesn't mean you need to be perfect when you come out." There is no shame in asking others for help along this journey as well.

All in all, it's important to remember that God is not in the "storms" and "earthquakes" of our lives. He is not orchestrating the calamities that we face. Instead, God can be found in the still and quiet voice that offers us hope and encouragement for the future. Take time—like Elijah—to pick out that voice, and you will come to know a new measure of peace. Remember the passion that you had for your calling when it was first given to you, and you'll find the strength to carry on even when you feel lost.

As a review, here are some of the main objectives we talked about in this chapter:

✝ Focus on caring for others rather than dwelling on your own problems

✝ Look for tangible, practical ways to build other people up

✝ Reframe your mentality to focus on positive, uplifting thoughts

✝ Use your pain to find common ground with others and to encourage them

✝ Always lean on God for comfort and strength!

Receiving and developing your vision is one thing, but what about the long term? Unfortunately, life often gets in the way of all our best-laid plans, chipping away at our passion with little discouragements and distractions. If you want to bring your vision to fruition then you must strike a balance between keeping your eyes on your ultimate goal and adapting when circumstances change. This skill is one of the most distinctive marks of a great leader.

Mike Robbins understands how hard it can be to actualise your vision. As the senior pastor of New Creation Church in Newquay and Redruth, Cornwall, Mike has spent the past two decades spreading his own vision of a charismatic, globally-minded church in the area. He's also a con-summate encourager, who's passionate about seeing the church reach its full potential and helping each individual believer fulfil their ultimate purpose for the Lord.

I recently had a fantastic conversation with Mike about the various struggles he has overcome to make his vision a reality. In this chapter, I'll follow Mike through his career and ministry to point out some of the things that his journey can teach us about spreading our vision to others.

PRINCIPLE #1: *CLARITY*

The first truth of adaptability is a somewhat ironic one: if you want to learn how to change, then you need to know what *can't* change. You must have a solid grounding in your purpose and faith. That way, when you do need to make changes, you won't be blown so far off course that you lose sight of your original call. You will always have an anchor to hold you steady. What will define you in the years to come, when situations have changed?

I believe that there are three major areas that you must use to "anchor" yourself and your team:

✠ Biblical principles: "The only thing that doesn't change is the word of God," Mike said. God's promises and character will never change, no matter what else may happen.

✠ Your ultimate goals: Cling to the original vision that God gave you. Though its appearance or impact may change through the years, it will come about in some form. God brings His plans to the world, without fail.

✠ Your organisational values: "I believe God is systematic and strategic," Mike said. "Being led by the Spirit doesn't mean that we're not strategic." Principles like honesty, integrity, and compassion will never go out of style. No matter what your business or ministry faces in the future, Godly values will make you stronger.

"Discovering vision and then formulating a strategy that sees that vision through is essential," Mike said. "Vision is born in a furnace. We need to engage with God. We have to discover God's heart. We need to clearly define who we are, so people know what they're joining up to and understand where we're going. People rise to vision. If they can sense that vision and anointing, they buy into it." Only once you and your team are firm and united about the three areas above can you begin to lead others. If you don't believe whole-heartedly in the value and importance of your mission, then you can't expect others to come on board.

PRINCIPLE #2: PATIENCE

But Mike Robbins wasn't always the competent, Spirit-filled pastor he is today. "I'm an aerospace engineer by trade," Mike said. "I lived a wrecked life. I'm a first-generation Christian, I did the drinking thing and lived with my girlfriend for quite a few years. I was quite insecure in those days. But eventually, we found Christ. We were both saved out of a very chaotic background."

As we can see, it took literal years for Mike to accept God's call on his life. Likewise, we all need to remain patient, both about our physical circumstances and our spiritual growth. Remember: no great leader has been built in a day. "When I came into ministry," Mike said, "I had to spend a lot of time sorting out who I was, the real guy Jesus had created. I had to discover him and allow him to emerge." Mature leaders give themselves time to grow.

Even after we have our own motives sorted out, the world rarely bends itself to our wishes. In fact, Mike spent eight long years after his initial call to ministry waiting for God to provide the right opportunity. During that time, Mike continually felt as if circumstances had been orchestrated against him: he was repeatedly denied positions, passed over for ministry jobs, and told that he wasn't qualified because of his background. "I knew I was called after three years, so I applied for Bible College," Mike said. "I kept trying to knock on that door to get into ministry, because I knew God had called me. Each time I got a knock back, for one reason or another, until eventually He came and got me." Eventually, Mike's church reached out and asked him to take on an assistantship role.

Somewhat ironically, that call came when Mike's engineering career was finally taking off, and he wasn't sure if he had the credentials to lead. "I had no Bible training at all," he said. "When I'd been invited, I approached the movement and asked 'Will you credential me?' And they said no, because I hadn't been through college. I got quite bent out of shape over it. God really pulled me up on that, and said 'It isn't about credentials.'" A few busy years later, Mike was planting a new church of his own, at the request of the board that had initially turned him down.

Don't be surprised when your dream isn't adhering to the timeline you originally envisioned. God often gives us a "big picture perspective," like He did when He showed Mike that he'd be a pastor in the years to come. He chooses to give us this ultimate vision so that we will have faith during difficult times, not to show us exactly what will happen within the next calendar year! If it seems like your vision is stalling, it doesn't necessarily mean that you've chosen the wrong course—just that God is working out some of the smaller details behind the scenes.

As we read in the book of James:

Be patient, then, brothers and sisters, until the Lord's coming. See how the farmer waits for the land to yield its valuable crop, patiently waiting for the autumn and spring rains. You too, be patient and stand firm, because the Lord's coming is near.

—JAMES 5:7-8

No one likes to wait. And in our fast-paced society, we are accustomed to getting what we want when we want it. But God's timing is far superior to the world's timing! So instead of panicking when things aren't moving quickly, enjoy the slower pace and trust in God's perfect knowledge and providence.

PRINCIPLE #3: *FLEXIBILITY*

Great leaders stay on their toes. They understand how to adapt to new and challenging situations. They always rise to the occasion, even when it's something they did not anticipate. Difficult financial trials, messy personal conflicts, and a whole range of other unforeseen circumstances can all present a challenge for the Christian leader.

"I'm bi-vocational now," Mike said. "I had to learn on the hoof and do my studying while I was running a church. To keep the staff and team going, we've had to make some alterations." He actually went back to work as an engineer in order to lighten the financial load on his church. At one point, he was working three days a week as an engineer, running the church, and studying ministry practice—all at the same time! If you want to grow into a big vision, then you will need to cultivate the same level of flexibility and sacrifice in your own personal life.

Sometimes, flexibility means having the courage to point out when something isn't going well. This is a conversation that never gets easier! You may risk offending, disenfranchising, or alienating others, especially those who you are working with closely. But it's a crucial step toward progress.

"The first step of a leader is to define reality," Mike said. "We have to say 'This isn't working. It has to be better than this.'" I put a big book

45

for people to put in words or pictures and everything they saw and felt. Then I took the book into a room and prayed through the whole lot and asked God to show me where He wanted us to go. From there, I produced a document called 'Who We Are.' It described, to anybody who was going to join our church, why we do what we do." Even further, Mike developed a three-hour seminar to help prospective members understand his church's mission, values, and statement of faith. As a result, the church saw its numbers soar—all because Mike was willing to admit that a strategy wasn't working.

PRINCIPLE #4: RESILIENCE

One mistake that driven, ambitious leaders often make is mistaking a course correction for a failure. We have a concrete, precise idea of exactly how we want our careers and ministries to turn out, and we do our very best to make that idea a reality. It's why we're effective leaders in the first place! However, this mentality can damage us greatly as well. Sometimes, when we feel like we've gone off track, we begin to let go, thinking we have failed.

Often the course correction comes from God Himself, as a response to our pride or undue ambition. "I came into a church with all the solutions to all the problems in the world," Mike recalled of his early days in ministry. "I was the next Billy Graham! I came here to cut my teeth on the place and figure out who I was, and then I'd get invited to a bigger church. That was in my head." But over the next two years, Mike began to sense that maybe God was calling him to remain in his current position.

At a ministry conference, that sensation sharpened into a message that was impossible to ignore. "I can remember in the vision that I saw that day the altar of Elijah," he shared, "and on it I saw selfish ambition. I can remember saying, 'That's just nonsensical!' but the moment I tried to move I heard the Holy Spirit say very clearly: 'Stay where you are. You need to deal with this.' It just smashed me," Mike recalled. "I ended up in a real snotty mess, but probably in the best state I've ever been in my spiritual life. Have a nervous breakdown — I recommend it!" In that moment, Mike needed a serious course correction. He needed to reposition his motives and attitude in order to best move forward.

Sometimes, however, these course corrections come as a result of outside circumstances. At one point, Mike's church lost a large number of members because of some changes that he had put into place. "Satan played mind games with me," he said. "When those people left my church, all I could hear was, 'You're the wrong person, you've blown it, there's someone better than you out there.' All those voices coming in began to cripple me because I wasn't convinced that I was the right person—which was ridiculous, because I came here because I knew God had called me!"

Imagine for a moment that you're baking a beautiful cake. You gather all the ingredients—the flour, the eggs, the sugar—and mix them all together in the bowl, and then you pour the whole mess into the pan. Does the cake ever look beautiful at that stage? Of course not. Most of the time, it doesn't even look edible! Or imagine a rocket en route to a distant star. Is it always pointed directly toward its destination? Certainly not! In fact, it sometimes doesn't even look like it's on course at all. But without those intermediate steps, baking a cake or reaching other worlds would be completely impossible. The same is true of our leadership journeys. So many of the things that we mistakenly view as "messes" or outright "failures" are actually just the intermediate stages of our vision.

When you're discouraged about changing courses, then take some time to remind yourself of why you're passionate about this vision in the first place. Revisit the scriptures that stuck with you when you first received your call. Speak again with the mentors and friends who encouraged you to pursue your vision, and pour out your questions to God. And above all? "Be confident in Christ," Mike advised. "Knowing that He's with me and has called me here helps me to bulldoze through those obstacles. I know I'm the right man. I can succeed, I can fail, but the reality is this: I am the right person in this place."

To review, here are some of the key concepts that we've reviewed in this chapter:

✟ Anchor yourself to Godly promises, values, and objectives

✟ Be patient and trust in God's power when plans slow down

✟ Adapt to new situations and don't cling to strategies that aren't working

✟ Don't confuse a course correction with a mistake

Chapter 5 | BIGGER THAN YOU

So what?

You've built and communicated a vision. You've endured through dis-couragements and setbacks, and kept pressing on even when times got tough. You've shared your vision with passion and grace. At the end of all this work, we often find ourselves asking one pesky, troubling question: "Was it worth my time?"

If your vision truly came from God and was blessed by Him, then the answer to this question is almost always an emphatic "Yes!" Sometimes, however, it's difficult to feel that optimism in our hearts. We may not see the full effects of our efforts, since a truly compelling vision's influence will endure far beyond our lifetime. But how do we ensure that our vision reaches beyond ourselves?

To get some insight into these hard questions, I spent some time talking with Jon Gordon. Jon has an impressive business résumé: he has worked with clients as diverse as West Point Academy, Northwestern Mutual, and Southwest Airlines, as well as many others. He's also written a multitude of excellent books, including *The Energy Boss* and *The No Complaining*

Rule, both of which spent long weeks on national bestseller lists. Above all, however, Jon considers himself a servant and follower of Christ. He is passionate about loving others with intention and finding ways to share a message of optimism and hope with everyone around him.

In this final chapter, with the help of Jon's wisdom, I hope to show you some of the main characteristics of a truly long-term, revolutionary vision.

PRINCIPLE #1: *IT'S PERSONAL*

Jon's entire life has enabled him to empathise with people who feel spiritually lost and discouraged. "I grew up in a Jewish-Italian family. A lot of food, a lot of guilt. A lot of wine, a lot of whining," Jon joked. "But we never went to church or temple. I was a seeker throughout my twenties and early thirties."

Later, Jon experienced a very stressful period in his life, when his marriage was struggling, his career was faltering, and he felt utterly lacking in purpose. "My wife was tired of my negativity," he said. "I opened up a burrito place so that I could fund my writing and speaking. And two weeks before the restaurant opened, I lost my job. I didn't have insurance for my kids, didn't know how I was going to pay the bills. It was during that time that I said, 'What was I born to do? Why am I here?' I wanted to live this life that I was meant to live."

During that time, Jon could never possibly have envisioned how this pain would help him to relate to others. God gave Jon exactly the kind of experiences that would allow him to empathise with others going through periods of turmoil. Jon could have easily let his personal background shape him with bitterness and anger. But his intimate relationship with God allowed him to see the deeper value behind his pain.

A personal conviction can only come from one place: a passionate and transformational relationship with our Father. "You can't know your purpose without a relationship with the One who created you for a purpose," Jon shared. "God has you here for a reason. It's up to you to say 'Use me, I'm open! Show me what you want me to do. Make me an instrument of your peace and love. Make me a vessel for your Holy Spirit. Make me a conduit for the miracles you want to see in the world.' If you're open to that, then God uses you. That spiritual transformation changed my heart, my soul, everything about me. In the past, it was all about me. But having Jesus in my heart changed me from the inside out." See, God gave Jon exactly the kind of experiences he needed to be grounded in purpose.

Everyone wants to be transformed. We can see this fundamental desire in our society's obsession with everything from fad diets to self-improvement seminars. This is just a manifestation of our God-given desire for renewal, which can only be fulfilled through a connection with the God who gave you that desire! Is your relationship with the Lord a core aspect of your being? Do you continually look for the empathy-growing experiences He has given to you?

PRINCIPLE #2: *IT EXCEEDS YOU*

Just because your message is personal doesn't mean that it should be exclusive to you. A powerful and inspired vision has the ability to grow beyond the limits that we impose upon it. Jon started out small. He began by sending out daily encouragement emails to friends and acquaintances, then moved on to giving free speeches at various venues. From there, he started to write bestselling books. But Jon's passion always revolved around others rather than himself, and his passion seemed almost bigger than he could contain. "For me," he said, "it was about speaking everywhere and anywhere to share the message that I had inside of me."

Jon frequently fields questions about his future prospects, especially since his last few books have seen such great success. "People ask what I want to do five years from now," he said. But he thinks of this question as a distraction from his true purpose, which is to touch as many people as he can in as lasting a way as possible. "When I die, hopefully a while from now, but even if it were tomorrow," he said, "someone meets my children and says to them, 'Hey, I read your dad's book, and it made a difference in my life.' To me, that's success. I live every day with that end in mind. That out of everyone I interact with, hopefully I'm inspiring someone."

In the end, that should be our own measure of success. Our visions should be revolutionary and life-changing enough that we cry out to God for his help in carrying them out. Ask yourself these questions:

✟ In what ways am I challenging the status quo? Am I encouraging others to think in a new way?

✟ Am I using my words and actions to combat injustices that I see in the world?

✟ Does my message undermine harmful stereotypes and social norms? Do I help people to see the true potential in themselves and others, especially the potential that society denies them?

"It's going to be a struggle, it's going to be a grind," Jon said. "But if you love others and you invest in them and make them a priority, as you help them grow you will grow. As you serve others, you improve as a leader. Ironically, when we help others we help ourselves. We grow into the leaders that God has called us to be." Is your vision big enough that you know you could never do it without God's help?

PRINCIPLE #3: *ITS MESSAGE IS TIMELESS*

Why have Jon's books and events resonated so powerfully with so many people? In part, it's because he offered an understandable message that everyone—regardless of their age or background—could easily relate to some point in their lives.

Let Jon explain his ministry's ideology in his own words: "The core message was positivity, choosing to be positive in a world of negativity," he told me. "Having faith and always moving forward. Not Pollyanna positive, and not the kind of positive thinking we do on our own, but moving forward in the face of adversity and setbacks. It's really about grit. That's what moves us forward to ultimately be our best and to bring out the best in others."

Powerful, right? It's a succinct yet moving mission statement, universal enough to resonate with a lot of people but specific enough to be unique. It applies to everyone (after all, who couldn't use a bit more grit in their lives?), but Jon's focus on love and service gives it a different perspective from the world's idea of positivity. In sum, Jon said something everyone needs to hear in a way that no one else was saying it.

And that's the best way to craft a message that truly inspires a large number of people. As Christian leaders, we don't want to build a vision that disappears alongside all the other messages out there today. Rather, we should inspire others to study and learn more about God. We should compel them to examine themselves and open themselves up to sacrificing for the Kingdom. By encouraging others to take up our message and pass it on further, we enable it to grow in an exponential fashion.

PRINCIPLE #4: *IT LIVES BEYOND YOU*

One of my favourite examples of a long-term, compelling vision comes from the book of 1 Chronicles, when God granted David a glimpse of the Temple that would be built for the Israelite nation. I believe that this narrative should be carved into every Godly leader's heart, shaping the way that we think about our calling and our place in God's larger plans.

David had expressed a desire to build a beautiful place of worship in Jerusalem, and the prophet Nathan assured him that the Temple was God's will. Then we read this:

> *But that night the word of God came to Nathan, saying: 'Go and tell my servant David, 'This is what the Lord says: You are not the one to build me a house to dwell in.*

—1 CHRONICLES 17: 3-4, NIV

That had to sting! Rather than becoming bitter that he would never see the Temple God had shown him, however, David offered up a prayer of thanks:

> *And now, Lord, let the promise you have made concerning your servant and his house be established forever. Do as you promised, so that it will be established and that your name will be great forever. Then people will say, 'The Lord Almighty, the God over Israel, is Israel's God!'*

—1 CHRONICLES 17:23-24, NIV

Much of the time, we feel like a failure if we don't see our plans come to fruition during our lifetime. On a certain level, that impulse is totally understandable: there's nothing wrong with wanting to see the results of our hard work and dedication. But sometimes a vision's longevity is actually the measure of its greatness. The Temple was one of the most important institutions of Israelite culture: it was the heart of the people's spiritual life, the issuance of God's voice, and a beautiful foreshadowing of Christ's future work in our hearts. Count yourself uniquely blessed if you have been given a vision of similar scope and range.

"It's impact, it's producing a harvest, it's planting a seed," Jon said. "You may not see the result, but you truly believe and know that a harvest is coming down the road. Somehow, someway, God will produce it. It's not about you getting recognition or reward." The vision bestowed on you may not see fulfilment during your generation, or for many generations yet to come. That means that it is a revolutionary idea!

"I believe that God doesn't pick the best," Jon told me. "He picks the most willing. If you're willing, He'll mould you and shape you to make an impact and do His work. I believe that comes from knowing your purpose." Have you made yourself available to God? Have you followed His will? Have you trusted Him with your life? Then you can rest knowing that you have made the impact God envisioned for you. In the end, the fulfilment of your vision lies in God's capable hands. When you've done all that you can, rest in the knowledge of His perfect will.

As a review, here are the principles we've discussed for ensuring you're your vision has a lasting legacy:

✟ Your vision is drawn from your own experiences and is personally meaningful to you

✝ Your vision grows out of a transformational relationship with God

✝ Your vision is powerful enough that you need God's help to see it through

✝ Your vision conveys a message that is both universal and unique

✝ Your vision is wide and encompasses generations

The ability to create and manage wealth

Chapter 6 | GETTING YOUR HOUSE IN ORDER

One of our primary goals as leaders is usually to make sure that our organisation is financially secure and thriving. In their haste to solve their organisation's money troubles, however, many leaders make a huge mistake: they neglect attending to their own personal financial situation.

Why does this present such an issue? After all, shouldn't the leader's primary focus be directed toward the funds and people that they are responsible for at work? Of course! But not even the most effective leader can perfectly divorce their personal life from their business or ministry. The simple fact remains that the habits you create at home will follow you into your ministry or workplace. If you are irresponsible with your personal income, you will be irresponsible with your organisation's funds as well—and vice versa.

It's important, then, to consider our personal attitudes toward money and to carefully think about the ways that we manage our finances at home. Devin Thorpe is one of the most financially literate people with whom I have ever spoken, but his ambitions are far greater than simply learning to manage money well. I interviewed Devin for episode 38 of *The Rising Generation* Podcast. Devin likes to think of himself as a "champion of social good." When we spoke Devin gave me some solid advice about how he manages his own personal finances, as well as sharing his thoughts on global ministry.

During his long and productive career, Devin has worked as an investment banker, CFO, treasurer, mortgage broker, and a member of the United States Senate Banking Staff. And as the founder of *'Your Mark on the World'*, an organisation that works to provide information and empowerment to young financial professionals, Devin understands the challenges unique to setting and achieving your goals. Overall, he is passionate about studying the ways that we can use financial principles to make an impact on some of the world's biggest social issues, and spreading that knowledge on to others.

Devin sees his work in finance as inspired by and empowered by his faith in Christ. He believes that financial stability and bold entrepreneurship can help solve huge social issues like cancer research, homelessness, and global poverty. He has written many books on these topics, including *'Crowdfunding for Social Good'* and *'Your Mark On The World'*, and has spoken all over the world about topics related to:

✝ Adding Profit by Adding Purpose

✝ Building a Movement to Change the World

✝ Crowdfunding for Social Good

As a contributor to Forbes Magazine, Devin covers issues like investment and entrepreneurship, focusing on the ways that young leaders can bring positive social change to their communities.

Though Devin's ultimate goals are global, he is adamant that you can only achieve this kind of radical change when you are in control of your own individual circumstances. Being financially secure gives you the stability you need to change the world.

PRINCIPLE #1: *THINK BIG, START SMALL*

Devin is passionate about young leaders, whom he believes are more focused on solving global problems and serious social issues. The reason why Devin chooses to motivate and train young entrepreneurs is that they're not afraid to make a bold first step in pursuit of their personal and financial goals.

What can the rest of us learn from these inspiring young innovators? "I think the key bit of advice is just to start doing something!" Devin said. "It sounds simple—it sounds overly simple—but there is so much that you will learn by just doing something to solve a problem. As you start doing something and accomplishing milestones, you're going to naturally draw other people into your sphere."

When one person chooses to change a part of their life, that decision can have a powerful ripple effect on others' decisions. As Christian leaders, we have been blessed with the gift of influence. Our good example has the potential to inspire and motivate many other people. Personal responsibility is the most natural and effective way for us to set a positive example for others. If the people under your influence see that you approach your personal finances with integrity and wisdom that will motivate them to embrace those same principles in your business or ministry.

What are some of the small financial decisions that could make a big difference in your life? Here are a few ideas:

✝ Cut out one "luxury" expense (like daily coffees or magazine subscriptions)

✝ Cook more at home rather than eating out

✝ Make more than the minimum monthly payment on your credit cards

✝ Call your phone or Internet provider and see if you can negotiate a lower rate

Now imagine that everyone in your organisation or business made those kinds of decisions too, and how many lives could be changed as a result. Furthermore, think of what could happen if everyone brought those same ideals of financial responsibility to work with them every day. The impact could be tremendous! Remember that you set the standards of behaviour for the rest of your team. And the movement created by one person's small decision has the ability to change the world. "But it all starts with that single effort," Devin shared. "It creates its own momentum."

PRINCIPLE #2: *PLAN FOR THE FUTURE*

Even though Devin has many skills and successes to his name, he gives all the ultimate credit for his success to faith in Christ. "My faith has been vitally important to me," he shared. "I draw tremendous strength from it." Clearly, Biblical principles ought to make up an integral part of our money philosophy.

Over and over again, God's word tells us that saving money is a crucial part of Biblical living. A healthy habit of saving is actually the foundation upon which all the other elements of stewardship can be built. After all, how can you invest responsibly or help others if you don't know how you will provide for yourself in the long term?

In the following passage, the book of Proverbs gives us a wonderful picture of Godly stewardship in nature:

Ants are creatures of little strength,
yet they store up their food in the summer.

—PROVERBS 30:25

Many passages from Proverbs are quite enigmatic, but this one is easy to figure out: God's creatures naturally know that they must work hard when work is plentiful in order to save up for more difficult times. Devin stresses that managing your spending is the key to saving responsibly. If you try to grow your investments without paying attention to how much you spend day to day, you'll always be a step behind. As they say: you need to spend well to save well.

So make an effort to keep tabs on your spending. Make a monthly budget and stick to it. Work on paying off your outstanding debts. Don't spend money that you don't need to, and pray about major purchases. Take some time to evaluate which items are actual necessities, and which are merely luxuries. Forcing yourself to consider whether or not you actually *need* the item you're about to purchase can revolutionise your spending habits for life.

PRINCIPLE #3: *BALANCE WORK AND REST*

Dedicated work is important, but it is certainly not the only element of a healthy financial attitude. Sometimes, in fact, it can even stand in the way of your goals. Many people—especially those of us in positions of influence—fall into the trap of thinking that if they just work a little bit longer or a little bit harder, they will solve their financial problems. This attitude prompts many late nights and unhealthy patterns of overwork, and it's the reason why so many otherwise fantastic leaders aren't living up to their full, God-given potential.

Here are some of the scientific benefits associated with regular periods of rest:

✟ Less stress—people with lower stress levels also have healthier hearts, lower blood pressure, and better sleep schedules.

✟ Creativity—people who regularly take time off to rejuvenate are less overwhelmed by their problems and find it easier to come up with solutions.

✟ Perspective—time off sharpens your mind and reset your focus, so that you're even more effective when you return to work.

✟ A healthier mind—people who embrace relaxation are less likely to suffer from negative mental states like depression and anxiety.

You see, this attitude of "all work, no play" just isn't God's plan for His people. As an example, just think of a time when you felt particularly burnt-out. Did you feel like you were fulfilling God's plan for you in that moment? Hard work and dedication are certainly important elements of Christian character and personal success, but we simply were not made to work around the clock.

> *There remains, then, a Sabbath-rest for the people of God,*
> *for anyone who enters God's rest also rests from their works,*
> *just as God did from His.*

—HEBREWS 4:9-10

If you want to have a genuinely productive, healthy attitude toward your work, you absolutely must balance it with periods of physical and spiritual rest. This is a somewhat counterintuitive idea, and it goes against the grain of our workaholic modern culture. It may seem like taking time off will hurt our overall productivity, but the situation is actually the exact opposite: rest helps us to get rid of stress, gain new insights about our problems, and approach our work with a renewed passion once we return to it.

PRINCIPLE #4: *GIVE GENEROUSLY*

151

Once you've stabilised your own financial situation, you are in a position to help others. Generosity is the best kind of financial precedent for the Christian leader to set for the people under their influence. In his letters to the Corinthian church, the apostle Paul praised all the believers who sincerely loved to help others with gifts of their resources:

> *Each of you should give what you have decided in your*
> *heart to give, not reluctantly or under compulsion,*
> *for God loves a cheerful giver.*

—2 CORINTHIANS 9:6-7

The great joy that comes from generous giving is available to every believer. Christ blessed those who gave shamelessly despite their own difficult financial situations, and the Bible repeatedly praises the generous poor. So there is no excuse for not sharing our blessings with those in need.

Of course, there are as many different ways to give as there are people in need of help. Many people of faith choose to tithe the traditional ten percent of their income, while others prefer to support people and charities as God calls them to do so. It is your responsibility to choose what will work best for you and your family.

The amount and the manner in which you give, however, is far less important than your attitude. God rewards those who give without bitterness or complaint. Providing for those who are less fortunate is hardly a burden—rather, it is our privilege as God's representatives in this world. Let your attitude toward charitable giving reflect that truth.

The influential theologian and preacher John Wesley once famously declared: "What should rise is not the Christian's standard of *living*, but his standard of *giving*." Providing for others should be one of the Christian leader's most important goals. Look for ways to bring God's love to the world through your finances, either on an individual level or through your organisation.

PRINCIPLE #5: *KEEP YOUR EYE ON THE PRIZE*

Everyone wants to achieve their personal finance goals, but not everyone sees those goals through to completion. How can we stay motivated to achieve the resolutions that we set for ourselves?

One way to gain insight on this topic is to examine how others have accomplished their goals effectively. Devin was personally inspired when he studied the eradication of polio.

He shared that when researchers and charities believed that they were close to eradicating polio, they stopped looking for new solutions. They lost their drive because they thought the job was as good as done. But in the long run, this meant that people all over the world continued to suffer. Only when those organisations renewed their efforts did they finally succeed in curing this terrible disease.

"People thought that if they just kept doing what they were doing, polio would sort of peter out. But it didn't. What they realised was that they had to make an extra-hard push." Even though discovering the cure for polio is extreme, Devin believes that this example illustrates a fundamental principle about personal financial responsibility: don't assume that your work is done, don't get complacent. You may need to evaluate the effectiveness of your strategy from time to time to see if it's really working for you and if there might be a better direction to take.

"The real effort to solve a problem is going to come at the end," he said. "You can't just coast across the finish line." In fact, the "home stretch" often requires twice the effort and dedication. It can be tempting to get complacent when your goal seems so close but you need to keep a fresh perspective.

Achieving your personal finance goals—whether to get out of debt, donate more to charity, or just stick to a budget—is going to be difficult. Many people promise that they are going to rethink their finances. But as soon as they realise how much dedication this resolution will take, they run out of steam and abandon the goals they had originally been so passionate about seeing through.

The movement created by taking in action in your finances has the ability to change your world. But, as Devin says, "it all starts with that single effort." That's a profoundly encouraging truth for the Christian leader.

To review, here are a few of the key concepts that we've discussed in this chapter:

✟ Remember that seemingly small actions can have huge impact

✟ Embrace Biblical financial principles

✟ Prioritise saving and planning for the future

✟ Keep track of what you spend

✟ Always give yourself time to rest

✟ Pay attention to your "standard of giving"

✟ And don't give up or get complacent when you're close to reaching your goals!

| TAKING THE PLUNGE

What bold financial step does your organisation need to take in order to thrive?

Something probably came into your mind when you read that question: perhaps a big financial decision that has the potential to grow your busi-ness, or an expansion that could radically grow your ministry's outreach potential. Anyone who has served in a ministry leadership position under-stands that making these kinds of choices can be extremely demanding. Both Dan Im and Neil Powell have had plenty of experiences in this area.

A renowned expert in global church leadership, Dan Im has worked to plant and grow congregations of all sizes across the world, from Vancouver to Korea. He is currently a teaching pastor at The Fellowship, a thriving multi-campus church located in Nashville, Tennessee.

In addition to his work in church planting, Dan is also an accomplished author and consultant. His book, *Planting Missional Churches: Your Guide to Starting Churches that Multiply,* is a pragmatic guide for mis-sionaries and church planters who want to maximise their impact. An accomplished scholar and pragmatic consultant, Dan has a passion for seeing churches thrive and make a difference in the communities in which they are situated.

Neil Powell is also an experienced church planter and outreach coordinator, having served as a UCCF staff worker in his home city of Birmingham and as the pastor of City Church, where he has served since 1999. Today, Neil works on the steering committee for the Midlands Gospel Fellowship. He's also a coordinator for 2020birmingham, a church-planting initiative that aims to plant twenty new congregations in the city by the year 2020.

It can be tempting to wait "just a little longer" before making the big financial commitment that will grow your business or ministry. We want to make sure that we are ready for the change. We want to wait until we know exactly things are going to work out, or until we are sure that everything will fall into place smoothly after the change is made.

Now, it's certainly always a good idea to exercise care when you're making a critical judgment about finances. As leaders, we have a critical responsibility to guide our organisations toward financial stability, a task which requires a great deal of prudence and sober judgment.

However, your business or ministry also trusts you to facilitate growth and success, which oftentimes means making risky decisions. God has not put you in your current position to keep the status quo! He wants you to step out in faith, make those bold decisions, and take responsibility for your actions. An overly cautious attitude toward decision-making often cripples organisations. It prevents them from living up to their full, God-given potential. How many big ideas or world-changing projects have never come to fruition or never reached their desired level of impact because the person God called did not have the conviction to follow through on that calling?

Through my conversations with Dan and Neil and study of the Bible, I've put together a list of essential decision-making principles.

Hopefully, these truths will help you develop a wise and Biblical approach to financial decision-making.

PRINCIPLE #1: INVITE GOD'S PRESENCE

Throughout the Bible, we can see hundreds of examples of people making brave, sometimes dangerous decisions to advance God's kingdom. I believe that we have a very powerful model for Godly decision-making in the example of Nehemiah.

As cupbearer for the Persian king, Nehemiah had a highly influential position in one of the most economically and militarily dominant empires in the world. However, once he heard about the destruction of the Temple, he was faced with a difficult decision: what was the best way to help his suffering brothers and sisters in Jerusalem?

Before Nehemiah even thought about asking God for help he interrogated some of the refugees from Jerusalem, making sure that he was adequately informed about the situation. Then he began to pray. First, he remembered his own failures in the past, along with the way that the Israelite people's bad decisions had led them to this point. Nehemiah also looked to the past for encouragement and instruction, recalling Moses' example of steadfast faith and the many ways that God had shown providence toward His people. Finally, he appealed directly to God for help and guidance, specifically petitioning Him for success in his decision- making:

> *Lord, let your ear be attentive to the prayer of this your servant and to the prayer of your servants who delight in revering your name. Give your servant success today.*

—NEHEMIAH 1:11

This amazing prayer gave Nehemiah the courage to make a very risky choice: asking the king of Persia to let him rebuild Jerusalem, an enemy city. Using this general decision-making model can give us the same confidence and peace, both about the small choices that we make every day and the big ones that have the potential to change lives.

What are some of the lessons that we as Christian leaders can take away from this powerful Biblical example?

✝ Be as fully aware of the situation as you possibly can, gathering information from others and considering all the variables. Making a big financial decision without having all the relevant information is the surest way to get into trouble.

✝ Consider everyone that the situation will affect. Ask yourself: will this benefit everyone in this organisation, not just me? Who reaps the rewards if this decision turns out well? Who suffers if it goes wrong?

✝ Study how similar situations have turned out in the past, either within your organisation or with others. Ask more experienced people for their advice.

72

✝ Last, but not least: always, always, invite God's presence into the decision-making process! He is the one who has charged you with your purpose and mission, so go to Him humbly and ready to be changed.

These principles are universally applicable in ministry or business. They offer insight whether you're deciding whether to invest in a new building for your church, whether to hire a new administrator in your organisation, or whether to expand your startup into a new city or market. So the next time that you're faced with a tricky financial decision, think about Nehemiah's example. Perhaps you, too, are being called to step out in faith and do something extraordinary for God's kingdom.

PRINCIPLE #2: *KNOW YOUR HEART*

Responsible leadership means not only thinking about how your decisions will affect yourself, but also about how those choices will affect everyone in your team, organisation, or ministry. In fact, one of the qualities that distinguishes a great leader from a merely good leader is prioritisation of others' needs and interests over their own. Above all, we should think about God's purposes and commands.

But even the wisest leader knows how easy it is to attribute our own ambitions and goals to divine purposes. When we structure our priorities around what we want to happen, rather than what God has envisioned for us, we risk making a selfish decision. How can you know for certain whether the calling that you feel is actually from God?

Neil Powell understands how critically difficult it can be to discern God's still, small voice amid the clamour of your own personal ambitions and dreams. In fact, he cites it as one of his greatest struggles as a Christian leader.

"I think the biggest challenge is knowing the motivations in my own heart, and the biggest danger for those of us involved in Christian leadership is wanting to do the right thing for the wrong reasons," Neil shared. "Often, we find that we are doing things to make a name for ourselves or find identity in the work that we do. Sometimes, in wanting to be a leader, we're just wanting to boost our own ego, or to prop up our self-esteem, or to be in a position of power or control."

Egotism and selfishness don't lead to good decisions, but faith does. Neil never anticipated to work as a church planter. But over time, as he listened to God's voice, he realised that he was being called to serve in domestic missions. An acceptance of this calling gave Neil an understanding of the way in which God's will unfolds in our life.

"Do things because you love the Lord Jesus and want to serve Him," he said. "Even the good work that we do can be a kind of idolatry.

Get pride and ego out of the way and get to serve God from a secure identity."

According to Neil, figuring out your own motivations isn't a once- and-done chore. "It's a daily task," he told me. "There's a constant need to spot that danger. Is your value and worth situated in Christ? If that is my identity, I'm liberated from the need to perform for the sake of my own ego or reputation. I can simply serve the Lord and get on with the work that I'm doing." Here are some questions to ask yourself in order to figure out where your motivations lie:

✞ If this decision leads to success, will I give the credit to Christ, to others, or to myself?

✞ Whose approval do I hope to gain in this situation?

✝ If this decision does not work out, will I be more concerned about the failure or its impact on my reputation?

Once you have the answers to these questions, you will have a better idea of the desires at work in your heart.

What are the best ways to cultivate this awareness of our own hearts? Neil recommends dedicated Bible study as the best way to examine your motivations and ambitions. He begins every morning with a focused time of scripture reading and prayer, which he says helps him to keep his thoughts turned toward God's purposes during the rest of the day. In addition, he makes an effort to spend time in fellowship with other Christians who can keep him accountable for his decisions. Neil believes that this approach will help anyone sincerely desiring to walk with God.

PRINCIPLE #3: *DON'T BOW TO FEAR*

There is no deterrent more powerful than fear of failure. As human beings, we are wired to be on the lookout for potential disasters— it's part of our DNA. But through Christ, God has called us to an existence that is higher, to a mindset that is based not on fear but on faith.

In the next chapter, we'll be discussing some practical ways to handle financial misfortunes. For now, though, suffice to say that a competent and confident leader does not let a fear of failure dissuade them from taking bold steps. Failure is not the end. In fact, as many of the leaders I have spoken with testify, it can be an incredibly valuable learning experience. So don't allow trepidation about failure to hold you back from taking that bold and faithful step in pursuit of your leadership calling.

Because of Dan Im's extensive work in church planting, he's very familiar with the doubts and fears that tend to pop up during big decisions. After all, what requires a bigger step of faith than starting a new con-gregation? Over the years, Dan has developed a simple maxim about financial decisions: just do it!

"There's this myth that we need to have more money, or we need to get more volunteers, or we need to have more people coming to our church before we can ever think about multiplication," Dan shared with me. But he isn't swayed by this particular way of thinking. "If you have that mindset, you can never multiply— because you will never have *enough* money or *enough* people," Dan said.

The "perfect time" for that big expansion or investment might never come. This is not an excuse to make rash financial decisions, but an exhortation to trust in God's provision. If He has called you to make a difficult financial choice, then have faith that He will give you the resources and tools that you need to follow through on your decision.

Chapter 8 | MAKING THE BIG ASK

You've figured out a general plan for your business or organisation's success. Now, you just need to figure out how to get other people on board. Asking people for cash—whether in the form of an investment or a donation—is one of the most challenging things about business or fundraising. It is, however, absolutely essential.

For those of us in business, there is no task more intimidating than trying to convince board members or investors that our next big project is a good call. This kind of "big ask" presents an even more difficult challenge in the ministry, where so many projects are funded by donations. For many people in the ministry, asking for donations is an uncomfortable necessity. Don't panic, though! There are practical strategies you can embrace in order to make this process less difficult.

As Christian leaders, we need to understand how to convey the pas-sion that we have for our ideas in a way that makes others want to be involved in them as well, whether through gifts of money, time, or skills. That means having excellent interpersonal skills: understanding the way that people think, speaking competently and persuasively, and having a good grasp of how to handle conflicts when they come.

Ivan Vickers understands the many unique challenges that come with creating wealth. I interviewed Ivan on episode number 13 of *The Rising Generation Podcast*. Ivan is an internationally-regarded expert in marketing and management and has helped many organisations achieve their true potential. With years of experience in the business world and a humble devotion to his Christian principles, Ivan is a gold mine of practical, Godly, financial advice.

Ivan's mission in life is to create one hundred millionaires: people whose success comes from their walk with Christ and dedication to responsible business practices. He's passionate about helping people walk in faith, build good business habits, and chart a course for success.

During our discussion, Ivan was happy to share some of the keys to success that he's discovered through the years. I hope that his advice will be useful to you as you figure out how best to fund your vision!

PRINCIPLE #1: *CHART YOUR COURSE*

You simply cannot expect your donors and investors to be excited about your goals if you haven't outlined them in detail for yourself! Ivan places a high value on what he calls clarity in business. "How much do you want to make?" he asked. "Then pick a number. By designing your future, you will start to aim towards it. Imagine sailing into the Atlantic without a map!"

You need a map of what you're trying to achieve, and you can only have a map if you have a destination."

✝ What do you want your business or ministry to look like in five years?

✝ How much money do you ultimately want to make?

✝ How many people do you want to reach with your ministry?

✝ What do you really want to achieve in this venture?

Pray about these questions. Write down your answers, draw a diagram, or record yourself speaking about your goals—anything that you can come back to in the future. By having this tangible record of your goals, you'll be charting a course for success in the years to come.

Even better, use these goals to draft an elevator speech: a thirty- to forty-second description of yourself and your goals. Explain your own experience and passion, your company's long-term goals, and how you are planning to take them there. This is an invaluable asset that proves useful in so many situations. You never know what potential connections are out there until you can speak about your goals eloquently to everyone you meet!

PRINCIPLE #2: JUST DO IT!

When I spoke with Michael Pink on episode 54 of *The Rising Generation Podcast*, he gave me some brief and blunt words about the challenges of making a big ask. With many years of experience in sales and business administration, Michael certainly understands how difficult it is to present your work to others. "I began in sales as a very young man—scared spitless!" he said. "I was terrified to get up in front of one person, let alone five or ten, and present anything."

Fortunately, Michael's advice on this topic is incredibly simple. "You do what you're afraid to do," he said. "Make yourself do it!" Now, approaching people with confidence doesn't mean being arrogant or resorting to scare tactics to get them to do what you want. All you need to do is believe that your cause is worth other people's time, interest, and money. That will give your request all the urgency it needs.

PRINCIPLE #3: *BE ATTENTIVE*

Once you've figured out your wider goals, you can move on to specific strategies to ensure success in your interactions. How can we ensure a positive response to our message? One of the biggest reasons why interactions go south is inattentiveness. People can tell when you're focused on them and when you're not giving them your full attention. This distinction often marks the difference between a successful meeting and a bad impression.

What's the single most important habit you can change in order to make a great first impression? According to Ivan, it's putting down your phone. He is shocked by the degree to which people ignore each other in favour of their personal devices. As he marvels: "You sit in meetings, and people are more interested in what's on their phones than the actual meeting!"

Instead of gluing your eyes to the screen, make eye contact with the person you're talking to. Have a relaxed, natural conversation, uninterrupted by constantly checking your phone. This can be a tough habit to break because so many of us don't realise we do it. But if you make an effort to truly focus on others, you'll get a much more positive response.

PRINCIPLE #4: *ASSUME RESPONSIBILITY*

So you've landed that perfect client or big-time donor. What happens if things just don't work out? Ivan said that one of his biggest challenges starting out in business was navigating the difficulties that arise when financial agreements fall through. "You end up with a client who either pays you late or goes bust, for whatever reason," he said. "And then the money side goes wrong— in other words, you owe more than you earn. The biggest challenge for me was being able to walk in faith."

In the wake of a broken agreement or financial disaster, many leaders try to deny their own responsibility. Ivan fell prey to this trap: "I had gotten it wrong," he said, "and I was trying to save face. I needed to admit that I'd gotten it wrong, that I'd miscalculated, that I'd broken my own rules."

How does Ivan recommend working through this struggle? "You get on your knees, you pray," he said. "That's the only way you can get through it." Denying responsibility prohibits you from developing better strategies. The faster you admit that you were wrong, the faster you can move on, avoid those mistakes, and build stronger relationships in the future.

PRINCIPLE #5: LOOK FOR COMMON GROUND

Another mistake that many people make when approaching potential donors or clients is to focus entirely on what benefit they want to receive from the partnership. Of course, you want the person that you're speaking with to understand that you're serious about your goals and have a plan for achieving them—but don't focus on those things to the exclusion of *their* interests.

Instead, talk about the ways that you can both help each other. Any successful partnership is symbiotic in nature: it offers both parties a distinct set of benefits. People are more interested in what your business or organisation can do for them than what they can do for you, so keep that in mind when crafting your next presentation.

PRINCIPLE #6: *ASK FOR HELP*

Ivan is frustrated by the multitudes of people who are reluctant to ask for financial advice or consult with experts. "Many people start their journey and they never ask for help," Ivan told me. "There's nothing wrong with paying for help! Take the money that you would have paid for your phone and go get some advice. That advice will multiply ten times—you can have ten phones!"

Perhaps you know someone who's had success in a business similar to your own. Or perhaps there's a financial consultant who could offer you valuable knowledge about an aspect of your business that you don't know much about. These mentors and experts have a wealth of knowledge to offer, so take advantage of their wisdom!

PRINCIPLE #7: *ASK QUESTIONS*

When you're speaking to someone, don't spend your time thinking about what you're going to say next. Instead, consider their words and think about questions you can ask them. "For me, it's not about what we know: it's what we don't know," Ivan said. "When we uncover the answer to some questions, we'll figure out that what we do know is rubbish."

In fact, asking questions is the best way to find out what the other person has to offer you. Perhaps they're willing to contribute more than you were going to ask them for, or have some valuable knowledge about the ministry opportunity that you're discussing—all things that you will never know if you don't take the time to ask genuine questions and listen to their answers.

PRINCIPLE #8: *HAVE CONFIDENCE*

Ivan believes firmly in the value of self-confidence. After all, how will others believe in the importance of your mission if they can't see that you're confident in your abilities? Confidence is a crucial element of trust.

But confidence can be difficult to develop, especially if you don't think that your ideas are strong or "You don't feel like you know enough," he said. "You don't feel strong enough." This is a feeling that every Christian will face at some point in their journey, but it shouldn't be your constant state of mind.

"Confidence is always a tricky one," Ivan said, "because the line between confidence and arrogance is quite a fine one. I think we need to be careful when we start down the journey of becoming confident that we don't become arrogant."

How does Ivan recommend cultivating confidence and not arrogance? By asking questions, practicing humility, and making yourself vulnerable. Let others see that you don't think you have all of the answers, and you will earn their trust and respect. "When you ask questions," Ivan said, "you'll find that arrogance disappears."

As a review, here are a few of the ways that you can work toward confidence when making a big ask:

✝ Make a plan for where you want to be five years from now

✝ Pay attention to the people around you

✝ Take responsibility and learn from your mistakes

✝ Don't be afraid to ask for help from mentors or experts

✝ Ask genuine, interested questions

✝ Have confidence in in your goals and plans—but always stay humble

Chapter 9

LOOKING TO THE FUTURE

Now that you've worked out a way to accumulate funds, it's time to start thinking in the long term. This can be the most challenging aspect of finances, especially since our culture trains people to think only of the "here and now" and to consider only those things which directly affect them. So many individuals and organisations barely get by financially because they fail to think about what will happen beyond tomorrow. It's much rarer to find someone who has a dedicated plan for where they want to see their business in five months, five years, or even five decades from now.

There's no one better to give advice about planning for the long haul than Rabbi Daniel Lapin, who has made a name for himself by applying traditional Jewish principles to modern financial theories. Rabbi Lapin, whom I interviewed on Episode 43 of *The Rising Generation Podcast*, is considered one of the most influential leaders in the Orthodox Jewish world, having written and spoken for years about the value of applying Biblical principles for financial success. Rabbi Lapin is adamant that these foundational principles, while rooted in the Orthodox heritage, are hardly exclusive—he believes that they are applicable across cultures, in both the ministry and in secular business.

Rabbi Lapin is also the founder of the Pacific Jewish Centre, an Orthodox synagogue in California that has become an epicentre of Judaism in the United States. He has authored several bestselling financial manuals, including the popular *Thou Shalt Prosper* and *Business Secrets from the Bible,* and is a sought-after speaker. Over the years he has addressed hundreds of conferences and government events, and has been a guest contributor to many prominent television and radio programs.

Rabbi Lapin is a man totally surrendered to God's calling. In particular, he feels a powerful call to combat secular culture in the United States and across the world, and to call attention to the rich stewardship heritage that the Jewish and Christian communities share. The curriculum he shares at his website, rabbidaniellapin.com, has helped thousands of families revolutionise their approach to finances and embrace a new future.

When I spoke to Rabbi Lapin, he shared a few of the fundamental principles that he teaches in his popular finance curriculum. All of these ideas are specifically relevant for leaders, so I'd like to share some of them with you here.

PRINCIPLE #1: *LOOK TO THE BIBLE*

If you're ready to extend your leadership thinking long-term, then you need to embrace what the Bible has to say. After all, the principles in God's word are timeless and eternal. What better manual for how to create a financial plan that lasts? A great Christian leader understands how to build a financial plan on Biblical truths in order to ensure success for years to come.

Just as a person can read a whole book about particle physics or karate without actually gaining a full understanding of the subject, however, many Christians read the Bible—particularly the Old Testament—without realising that its principles are still directly applicable to modern life. This is a big mistake.

"People make the mistake of thinking that the Bible is nothing but a simplified book of children's stories," Rabbi Lapin said. But that simply isn't the case. As he says: "There are more rules and regulations about money than on any other topic." It is our responsibility as leaders to search out these lessons and figure out the ways in which they apply to our organisations.

One of the powerful truths that Rabbi Lapin finds in the Jewish scriptures concerns the amount of time that it takes to make a big lifestyle change. "You go through the Bible and notice how long Noah's ark was on the mountain: forty days and forty nights," Rabbi Lapin told me. "How long was Moses on top of Mount Sinai? Forty days and forty nights. How long were the Israelites in the desert?

Forty years! Forty keeps on cropping up again and again."

What's the significance? Rabbi Lapin believes that it has something to do with transforming your destiny. In fact, in all of the examples above, each of the Biblical figures mentioned was undergoing some life-changing event or circumstance.

This is a great encouragement for the Christian leader. Since it can be very difficult to persevere along a difficult path when you're not seeing any results—especially if others are depending on your guidance—it's good to know that Godly resolutions will always bare fruits.

Not all the benefits of a long-term change will be visible at this time, of course. But Rabbi Lapin encourages leaders: if you can stay on track for a month, then you've laid the foundation for lifelong success. "This isn't about getting rich quick. It is about dramatically changing your income figures for the year. There's still enough time." Many of the changes that we've outlined in this book can be implemented quickly in a short amount of time, as long as you approach them with total dedication and mindfulness, but the results they provide will last a lifetime. There's no excuse not to start applying these principles today!

PRINCIPLE #2: *INTERNALISE TRUTH*

However, it's not enough to know just the philosophies of success. You also need to memorise and internalise these Biblical principles so thoroughly that they become a part of your typical thought process.

In order to illustrate this principle, Rabbi Lapin uses this example: "Imagine that somebody is on their way to a city that's known for having dangerous areas. In the airport bookstore, he sees a book that says *Self-Defense in 20 Easy Lessons.* So he buys it and reads through it one the plane".

"And sure enough, he's walking around the city one night and feels a gun poking through his ribs. A hand comes around him from the rear, and he says, 'Excuse me, I think that attacks from the rear with a gun were covered in Chapter 17, I just need to review!'

That's not going to work very well! What will work is investing the time and bringing the lessons of that book along the challenging 18 inches from the head to the heart."

For Rabbi Lapin, cultivating financial instinct is an incredibly important trait for those in a position of leadership. As a leader, you will frequently run into situations where you need to make quick decisions about money—and these are often decisions that affect many people besides just you and your team. The last thing you want to be doing in a high-pressure situation like that is scrambling for basic financial knowledge. You want that solid Biblical foundation to already be set.

PRINCIPLE #3: REINVENT YOUR MIND

This frequent exposure to and internalisation of the Bible can revolutionise our attitude toward money. "We have all been indoctrinated into believing that making money is evil, that it is the result of cunning and greed and conniving," Rabbi Lapin shared. We can see this in the commonly held belief that most rich people are immoral or unfair, or in many people's hesitancy to share their financial successes.

Unfortunately, this misconception traps us into thinking that our financial problems are a mark of our morality, or a sign of our virtue. We can start to believe that poor financial circumstances are a result of God's favour rather than the consequence that stems from our own bad choices.

Rabbi Lapin thinks that this is a particularly malicious cultural myth. "It's one of the main reasons that so many people who have it in them to prosper are fumbling and failing to achieve what they should," he said. This is an incredibly self-defeating thought process and it has the power to singlehandedly cripple your business or ministry.

As Christian leaders, we have a unique responsibility to combat this attitude in our businesses and organisations.

This requires getting it out of our own brains first! If you are a dedicated believer who thinks that acquiring wealth is sinful, then there will always be doubts about your own integrity in the back of your mind. You will simply never be able to lead your team to success.

PRINCIPLE #4: *LOVE WHAT YOU DO*

Another very persistent and distracting cultural myth at work in the mind of the Christian leader today is the idea that we must enjoy our jobs in order to find them fulfilling in any way. This kind of atti-tude pulls us away from learning to do God's work wherever He has chosen to place us. Instead, we spend our time worrying about whether we're really following our passion, and getting distracted by other opportunities.

"People are told all the time: 'You should do what you love, because then work will always be a pleasure,'" Rabbi Lapin said. "Well, I love bowling! And I have yet to find someone who will pay me a nice salary to go bowling. I just think it's a very damaging statement." Sometimes doing God's work requires a sacrifice. The great leader embraces these sacrifices for the sake of pursuing God's Kingdom.

Sometimes doing God's work requires sacrificing our own ambitions, either for a short period of time or for our entire careers. You can still have a fulfilling life without loving every aspect of your job.

God's system for financial success depends on overcoming personal preferences and focusing on His other children. Rather than thinking about your own desires and prospects, try to prioritise others.

PRINCIPLE #5: *KEEP TABS ON YOUR SUCCESS*

It's difficult to lose weight without regularly measuring your progress on a scale. In the same way, leaders must have a finger on the pulse of their organisations and businesses in order to determine how strategies need to be adjusted and altered over the long term. "If you cannot apply a metric to your goal, you will never achieve it," Rabbi Lapin shared. Somebody who wants to gain wealth and increase his revenue needs to be able to record it."

It's tempting to avoid taking an honest measure of our success because we're worried that the results might not match up with our goals—but that's just not a good enough excuse. You'll never reach those goals at all if you're not willing to take a hard look at your financial situation and reevaluate your strategy if need be.

"Somebody who wants to gain wealth and increase his revenue needs to be able to measure and record that," Rabbi Lapin advised. He recommends looking into the plentiful financial resources on the Internet in order to figure out the best way to keep tabs on your finances. Many of these resources exist, but it requires dedication. Turn off the television for a few weeks and dedicate yourself to reading and studying instead.

PRINCIPLE #6: *CHANGE YOURSELF*

The concept outlined in the last section may feel confining, especially since we've been trained our entire lives to "follow our dreams." But it's actually a very freeing truth. Once you're no longer bound to who you have been in the past, then you're free to determine who you will be in the future. We can embrace our identity as autonomous beings who have the power to change themselves. That's a huge part of being made in God's image!

"God created us with an ability to *become* deeply passionate about what we do," Rabbi Lapin said. "For all of us, there is a notion that we 'are what we are.' That's not how the good Lord created us. That's only true about animals."

So if you're not satisfied with your own job performance, or the performance of someone else on your team, then don't be discouraged: there's still hope! Find talking to people and negotiating difficult? "If you say you're not a 'people person,' get over it!" Rabbi Lapin said. "It's not a big deal." It is within your power to grow, develop, and better yourself.

PRINCIPLE #7: *THINK COMPASSIONATELY*

One of the principles that Rabbi Lapin emphasises the most is compassion and humble service. "Does God want us to be rich? Well, he hasn't shared that with me, to be honest," Rabbi Lapin said. "But what I do know is that He does want us to be obsessively occupied with the needs and desires of our fellow human beings. It doesn't surprise me that if we do that, we too will be blessed with the incredible blessing of financial abundance."

Whether your calling is to do good business or serve the world through ministry, make sure that you are delivering something of intrinsic value. Do work that betters the lives of others, and you will reap the rewards. In the Jewish tradition, material wealth derives naturally from service. So if you're struggling to achieve your financial goals, don't fall prey to get-rich-quick schemes or cut corners in the services or products that you provide in an attempt to turn a profit. That's the easy way out, and it won't pay off in the long term. Instead, ask yourself questions like these:

✟ Am I providing a quality product that improves people's lives?

✟ Are my products and services defined by quality? Do I ever cut corners or take advantage of people in order to make more money?

✟ Do my services actually increase my client's quality of life? Are my clients happier or healthier because of what I do for them?

✟ Does my organisation make a measurable impact on the world? Can I point to tangible situations where we made a difference to other people?

✟ If my business or organisation did not exist, how would the world be different? Would it be better or worse?

If your answers to these questions are in the negative, then maybe it's time to rethink your business model. As Christians, our primary mission in the world should always be to provide for others—all other concerns are secondary. Fortunately, this dedication to service often reaps plentiful rewards in the financial sector as well. It's our responsibility as leaders to make sure that our businesses and organisations adhere to this principle.

"All you have to do is take care of the needs and desires of His other children, and you will have all the money you could possibly need," Rabbi Lapin says. Your ultimate goal should be to improve the lives of others. This might be through providing a quality cleaning service, or fighting world hunger at your nonprofit organisation—but whatever you do, do it with integrity and decency.

Whatever your calling, make sure that you are delivering something of value. Do work that betters the lives of others, and you will reap the rewards. That's the kind of financial legacy that will last a lifetime.

To review, here are some of the crucial concepts we've gone over in this chapter:

☦ Embrace Biblical principles and apply them to your life

☦ Develop and practice using your financial instinct until it becomes second nature

☦ Don't buy into the lie that money is equivalent to sin

☦ Prioritise God's goals

☦ Keep a record of your finances and monitor what works well

☦ Work to better yourself and your team

☦ Offer something valuable to the world

3

The ability to defy
self doubt and lead
with conviction

| # WHO AM I?

One of the biggest struggles that we face as Christians and leaders is the question of our identity. We live in an identity-driven society, where everyone is obsessed with trying to answer questions like "Who am I?" and "What is my purpose in life?" Thankfully, as Christians we already have the ultimate answers to these questions: we are children of God, and our purpose is to seek His kingdom here in the world.

But it can be difficult to move that knowledge from our heads to our hearts, so to speak. Christians often struggle with the same kind of iden-tity crises as our neighbours simply because they don't apply this truth about themselves to their lives. If we want to have genuine confidence in God's plans for us, then we must have confidence in His purposes for us as well. This means situating our identities in Christ.

In one of my first interviews for this book with Yvonne Brooks, it quickly became clear that her identity is tied to her love for God. As a behavioural consultant, mental health nurse, assistant pastor of the New Jerusalem Apostolic Church, and founding director of the Women of Purpose Ministry, Yvonne certainly has a lot on her plate! Yet she consistently manages to invite joy and praise into her everyday life, a habbit that stems from her confidence in God's daily provision for her needs.

Yvonne is an internationally-sought after speaker and teacher. Her book on Christian living and discipleship, *Touching God's Heart: Prayers That Make A Difference*, have been a great encouragement to many as they walk with Christ. During the course of her career, she has received a number of accolades recognising the exceptional work she's done for the church, including the Women of Excellence Trailblazer Award and community service awards from the Association of Jamaican Nationals.

PRINCIPLE #1: *YOU ARE GOD'S CHILD*

If we are to become passionate followers of Christ, then we must think of ourselves as His brothers and sisters. It wasn't until Yvonne grasped this core principle that she glimpsed her own potential to do great things for the Kingdom. Her moment of awakening occurred during a leadership seminar: "The speaker began to talk about how, from the foundation of the world, God had created my purpose and created me to fit that purpose perfectly," Yvonne said.

"It was like a television moment—I was on my own in a building full of people. The message really came home for me that God saw me as an individual, that He had a plan for my life, that there was a purpose attached to me being here—that it wasn't just a random thing. It was like someone had thrown an incendiary device into my life!"

That fiery passion has motivated Yvonne through the rest of her ministry career. She looks back on it as a monumental turning point in her spiritual journey, and says that she still draws courage from the memory. It was in that moment that Yvonne realised that everything in her life had been directed by God in order to empower and enable her to succeed.

Yvonne realised that God had been continually by her side, guiding her to make the right decisions, showing her how to follow the right path in order to fulfil her purpose. "All through my life, I had a very strong sense of God's hand guiding me. In that moment, everything came together." A loving parent wants what is best for their child, and does everything they can to enable that child to succeed. That's how God feels about you!

Take a moment to look back over your life and thank God for His provision, during both the good times and the bad. You'll find new strength to approach your life with confidence, knowing that He's with you every step of the way.

PRINCIPLE #2: YOU ARE A SOLUTION

If we've been created for a specific purpose, then we don't have to be ashamed of the unique strengths and gifts that God has given us—after all, those are the things that will help us to succeed. The personality, struggles, and triumphs that God has given us help to make us unique and are shaped specifically to help us become who we were designed to be.

"The biggest challenge I have faced on an ongoing basis is the challenge to be myself," Yvonne said. "If you go back to the idea that God created me to fit my purpose perfectly, then obviously I am the answer to a problem! I am the solution to a situation. But if I don't know who I am and the abilities that God has given me, I cannot fulfil that purpose."

What's Yvonne's mantra for remembering her identity in Christ? "Know who I am, and be who I am, and don't feel the need to apologise for it." Don't feel like you need to compete with others around you who you think are better-looking, or more intelligent, or better liked. Instead, focus on your own identity as a valued child of God. Proactively seek out the problems and situations that your unique set of talents can help to solve. Perhaps you're good at working with young adults, or you are an effective public speaker.

God gave you those traits in order to be able to grasp the opportunities that life presents you, to make a significant contribution to the lives of those around you and for you to be able to fulfil your role in His grand plan.

These opportunities won't always drop themselves in your lap, especially if you lack the confidence to pursue them. So get out and explore the ways that you can bless the world!

PRINCIPLE #3: *YOU CAN DO THE IMPOSSIBLE*

Though Yvonne grew up in the church and was involved in ministry for her entire life, she never considered the possibility that she could make a living in the ministry. She remembers joking to a Sunday school teacher that she wanted to be a bishop when she grew up, never realising that such a thing could be possible for her. "I never expected to be in front-line ministry because I was a woman," she shared. "In those days, the woman was ministering to the pots and pans!"

Yvonne's humorous statement still makes a very valid point. For many years, she was unable to visualise herself in the ministry because the society around her said that dream was impossible. As Yvonne phrased it: "For a woman, there wasn't a route to success." In our society, many people—not just women—are told that they can't succeed.

What Yvonne realised later is that God does not often listen to society! In fact, many of God's most influential followers have been people who dared to challenge the status quo. Think about Biblical figures like Daniel or John the Baptist. These were people who stood up to cultural norms and brought about massive changes in their societies, all because they weren't afraid to follow God. We'll discuss strategies for making inroads into difficult working environments in our last chapter, but for now just understand that God desires for His people to break barriers and contradict society's expectations.

PRINCIPLE #4: *YOU CAN LEAD ANYWHERE*

Sometimes, however, God calls us to places that even we don't expect! He often requires us to serve in unglamorous or seemingly insignificant places. It can be easy for anyone, even those of us in leadership positions, to believe the lies we hear about service. These can be things like: "You can't minister unless you're a pastor" or "Full-time ministry is the only way to serve God." Even if we don't hear these messages directly, they still permeate Christian culture.

But Yvonne firmly believes that it is the Christian's responsibility to lead in the area where they've been placed, whether they think of that position as a traditional place of leadership or not. You don't need to be a pastor or a highly-paid conference speaker or a missions' leader to have radical faith in God and inspire others to follow Him. "If I'm a housewife with a family and a home," she said, "then I have to become a great leader. Unfortunately, we equate leadership with people like the President of the United States or the Prime Minister of the U.K."

We need to purge this idea about leadership from our minds. Sometimes, God calls us to lead in unexpected places. It's our responsibility to make the most of those surprises. "Your skills might not be in the pulpit or in public speaking," Yvonne said, "but you have power." And you certainly don't need to be called to full-time ministry in order to be confident that you have a unique purpose. Anyone who has a passion for service and for doing God's will is capable of doing great things for His kingdom here on Earth. So embrace where God has placed you right here and right now—you never know what blessings He has planned for you there!

PRINCIPLE #5: YOUR HABITS MATTER

But, you might be saying, what about our day-to-day routines? How can we embrace our Christ-like identity in each and every moment?

Yvonne is a huge proponent of daily routines, activities that remind us of our position in the Body of Christ. "It's the basic things, the little things, that make the difference," she said. "It's not the big things, like flying across the world or speaking to thousands of people. It's about the things you do before you even leave your house in the morning."

Neglecting these habits, small as they are, can be very damaging. As Yvonne says: "If your roots aren't down deep, then the stresses and strains and the pull of other people on your life will just yank you out of the ground." For Yvonne, being consistent in the word means three main things: prayer, journaling, and Bible reading.

Yvonne spends a few moments at the beginning of each day. "In the morning," she said, "I erect an altar of praise and worship." She does this by working through her Bible reading plan, listening to worship music, and meditating on some of the verses she's recently memorised. She takes a few moments to dedicate her day to God, and to pray for her family, friends, and for the global church. She allows God to bring specific needs and people that need her prayer to mind.

But she also tries to remain in that attitude of prayer throughout the day. "Prayer is our backdrop," she affirmed. "When I'm driving, God sits with me in the passenger seat. When I'm in the kitchen, I'm cooking—and praying! It's rejuvenating." You can cultivate this attitude as well. Just make an effort to bring God's presence to mind throughout the day, whether you're running errands or giving the dog a bath. Constantly remembering God's promises, whether through prayer or memorised scripture, is the best way to cultivate confidence in your daily life.

Yvonne also recommends journaling as a practical way to get in tune with God's presence. "After prayer, then I'll write my journal. I normally seek an agenda from the Lord for the day," she said. "I don't give Him my agenda. I give him the day and ask him to impose His agenda." It's important to plan our everyday lives—our meals, our errands, our habits—around God's plans for us. Try Yvonne's strategy this week: begin every day by sitting down and taking some time to pray and to journal your thoughts and prayers. Asking God for His agenda for your life for the day.

Hopefully, these principles have allowed you to see a more confident, faithful future for yourself. I hope that soon you can say, along with Yvonne: "I put my foot up on the edge, and then step up to take me over the edge—and by the time my foot comes down, there's ground under it!"

As a review, here are some of the concepts we outlined in this chapter:

✝ Embrace your identity as a child of God, and understand how much He cares for you

✝ Look for the problems that you were created to solve

✝ Don't be afraid to dream big

✝ Work to serve God in the position that you have right now

✝ Cultivate habits that remind you of God's presence in your life

Chapter 11 | HANDLING TRANSITIONS

We all know that it's easy to trust God when everything is going well. There's really no reason not to trust God if you're happy, healthy, and successful in your career. After all, the proof of His provision can be seen right in front of you! But what about when God's care isn't quite so obvious? How do you respond when God asks you to go through a major life change—perhaps a change that you didn't anticipate or desire?

Jason Alexander currently works as the executive pastor of Audacious Church, a groundbreaking worship centre in Manchester, where he believes that he's found God's unique calling on his life. He loves the city of Manchester, loves his job as a teaching pastor, and loves finding unique ways to give back to his thriving church community. Jason's passion is for helping others uncover their own individual purposes in God's plan.

Jason always had a sense that he was being called to dedicate himself entirely to the ministry and to building God's house. He took serious pay cuts and lived through many uncertain life situations in order to get to the ministry positions that he holds now. And then—the biggest challenge of all—God asked Jason to uproot his entire life. Several years ago, Jason and his family moved from Australia to Bristol in order to plant a church there. Though Jason now looks back on this transition as a positive one, because it gave him his job at Audacious Church, it was still a strain on him emotionally and spiritually at the time. This transition had the potential to seriously damage not only Jason's faith, but also his family's, yet Jason learned to navigate the difficult waters of change with confidence.

Jason finds a lot of encouragement during times of transition and tumult from Jesus' words in the Beatitudes. He used several of them during our discussion to illuminate some of the points he was making about leadership, faith, and the leader's responsibilities and struggles during a time of transition. I think the Biblical advice he shares is extremely helpful for leaders in business and ministry alike, and I'm excited to share some of it with you!

PRINCIPLE #1: *UNDERSTAND THE SITUATION*

"Transitioning from Australia to the U.K. was a big transition for us," Jason shared. "And so was handling that transition as a leader, going from close leadership relationships at the time to distant ones. And then transitioning from what was ten years of serving the senior pastor in the church there who was a father figure … to going onto a team with someone who was an older brother figure rather than a father figure. It's been amazing, but it's been a transition."

In this story, Jason pointed out a couple of areas in which transition can affect our lives:

✝ Relationships' change: Transition often entails making new relationships, leaving old ones behind, or changing our relationship focus

✝ Situations' change: Very few changes are entirely mental. They're usually accompanied by some kind of physical change, like a change of location or job

✝ Emotions' change: Your emotions will be volatile. You might feel sad, angry, or just confused

As a result of these factors, your role as a leader will also undergo a profound change during a time of transition. Perhaps you will need to step down from your position as a church worship leader, or move to a higher position in your company. This can give us a bit of an identity crisis, especially if we situate our identities in our leadership role.

When confronted with so many complexities, it's easy to get caught up in things that don't really matter. Jason admits that he has a huge distraction problem—he sometimes gets the urge to get a philosophy degree, or join a monastery! But he doesn't give in to distractions, and tries to focus on what he's called to do right now: "In that moment when there's a lot of things you could do, the thing to do is to quiet those distractions so you can see God," he advised. "Get clarity, so you're not just making up a pros and cons list and trying to navigate what the best thing is, but really go for what God wants for you."

Blessed are the meek,
for they will inherit the earth.

—Matthew 5:5

It takes genuine devotion and humility to sit down and examine what's going on in your life. So sit down and honestly evaluate how the change is going to affect you and the people around you. Try to look for positives in the situation. Don't get caught up in the little things that will change about your life—you'll get used to them in time, and they won't seem so bad. Instead, think about the big picture. See if you can find the ways that God might be working in your situation, then focus on those instead.

PRINCIPLE #2: *CAST YOUR CARES AWAY*

Jason reached a spiritual low point early in his marriage, when he was struggling both relationally and financially. He resisted the idea of surrendering all of his dreams and desires to God. "There was a real call from God to give everything over," Jason said. "And I thought at that point that 'giving everything over' meant giving over my time, my energy, my career choice and my life. But really, what I realised in that moment when I handed over to God, was I was giving him all my pain, all my hurt, all my disappointments. And He was lightening my load, not trying to burden me."

In the words of Jesus, God's yoke is light! He wants to see you thrive and flourish. Leaders are often very driven, ambitious people. We want to do great things. Sometimes, however, that drive to achieve can cause reluctance to hand any control of our lives over to God. We like to think that we know best. What Jason realised is that when we hand over our ambitions to God, we also hand over all our fears about our performance and the future. It was this profound realisation that healed Jason's relationship with God and began his journey toward the ministry in earnest.

God wants all of you: the shameful parts, the complicated parts, and the parts you like to hide from others.

Blessed are the poor in spirit,
for theirs is the kingdom of Heaven.

—MATTHEW 5:3

To be "poor in spirit" means to lay all of our cares and insecurities on God, which helps us know that He can work in even the messiest parts of our lives. Jason learned the hard way that God is invested in his whole being, not just his successes. "It was in that moment that I realised I could trust God with what the future was," Jason shared. "No matter how I could work it out in my own head … I could actually trust Him with all of the bad stuff, but I could also trust Him with the good stuff." Once we embrace the fact that God wants to work *with* our weaknesses, not *around* them, we can have a new confidence in His plans.

PRINCIPLE #3: *WELCOME ALL CHANGES —EVEN THE BAD ONES*

"In life, you transition," Jason said. "You go from being single to being married, that's a big transition. You go from being married to having kids, that's a big transition. You become homeowners, you have mortgages and career choice transitions. They all have an impact on you, I think."

Here's the important thing to understand: most of those transitions are welcome. Having kids, getting married, and buying a home—these are generally things that we do because we really want to do them. They're stages of life, not traumatic events. When does transition actually cause a problem? When it affects us in a way we didn't anticipate or desire.

109

Jason certainly knows how difficult a major life transition can be. After working in ministry for years, he's certainly lived through many of them. He said that the most difficult thing about a supposedly negative transition is that it can bring up a lot of doubts about your purpose and your behaviour. "If I was serving God here," it's easy to say, "then why would He put me somewhere else? Did I do something wrong where I was?" We can easily fall into believing that our change in situation is a punishment rather than an opportunity to serve God more effectively. Unfortunately, this doubt often leads people to stop following God's calling altogether.

> *Blessed are those who mourn*
> *for they will be comforted.*

—MATTHEW 5:4

It's perfectly fine to have doubts and fears about what the future may hold, especially if that future isn't what you expected it to be. But we shouldn't hold those fears inside, where they can fester and grow into anger. Instead, be honest about your struggles. Go to God in humble prayer and tell Him that you're unhappy or frightened about what He has planned—He'll lead you to the scriptures and people that you need. Sometimes other people can see the positives in a situation that you cannot, so find a spiritually mature friend or mentor who can listen to your doubts and provide encouragement for you. It may even help to use a personal journal and chronicle the things you feel about the transition. The most important thing is that you're talking about your thoughts and allowing others to speak the truth into your life. Open yourself to comfort during this difficult time.

PRINCIPLE #4: *SET THE STANDARD*

But Jason firmly believes that times of transition are valuable learning experiences for the Christian leader: "I think you build a depth and a strength of the weight that you carry as a leader when you handle transition well," he said. "Handle it well emotionally, handle it well spiritually, and handle it well for the people that you're leading. When people watch you in a time of transition it's a moment when the squeeze is really on."

The people that you lead are looking to you during any time of change or transition. It's our responsibility—and privilege—to be an example in times of trouble as well as times of happiness. During a transition, people look to those in leadership to set the standard for their attitudes

> *Blessed are those who hunger and thirst*
> *for righteousness, for they will be filled.*

—Matthew 5:6

Although the Beatitudes are meant to comfort us during times of trial, they certainly don't encourage us to sit on our hands when things go wrong! Instead, Jesus tells us to actively pursue virtuous living even in the midst of turmoil. Blessed are the people who go out and set a positive example, and blessed are the people who are proactive about their situations.

This principle can apply both directly and indirectly. Perhaps the difficult transition you're going through is one that directly affects your entire business or organisation. In times like this, those under our authority need leadership more than ever. It's your responsibility to model for your team members the best way to react to changes. For instance: if your business is suffering from some cutbacks, stay upbeat yourself and do your best to encourage others. This will foster an environment of support.

Or perhaps the transition is a more personal one that affects only you and your family. Even in these situations, be aware that the eyes of the people you lead are on you at all times, watching you to see how you react when to changes. You still need to behave with grace and wisdom. As an example, if you lose your job, let it be apparent to the people on your ministry team that you trust in God's provision. This kind of constant pressure can be very difficult to handle, but it's one of the most crucial responsibilities of being a good leader—and a Godly example to others.

PRINCIPLE #5: *SAY NO TO BITTERNESS*

Another of the traps that can ensnare us during a big transition is the growth of bitterness. Many people, even devoted Christians, can fall prey to this way of thinking. We are especially susceptible to this trap when the change is something that we didn't want to happen—such as an illness, an unexpected career change, or a move. "It's very easy when you're vulnerable," Jason said. "You're highly emotional, lots of things shift and change, you've got lots of opportunities to be offended."

They allow their anger about the situation to morph into bitterness, which isn't quite the same thing. Of course, anger may make us do unwise things in the heat of the moment—but bitterness is even more destructive. It grows over time, infects our heart, poisons our attitudes, and makes us distrust God's goodness toward us. We begin to believe that because one thing hasn't gone our way, the whole world—even the people who love us and Christ—must want us to fail. That attitude changes the way we behave every single day. We stop feeling compassion and joy. We stop valuing gentleness and kindness. This attitude has a powerful effect on the way we think and the way we lead.

Feeling genuine anger is not sinful, but allowing it to harden into bitterness and contempt toward other people can be incredibly damaging, both to our personal spiritual life and to our reputation as Christian leaders. Here's the Beatitude that Jason looks at in the times when he's tempted to give in to bitterness:

> *Blessed are the merciful,*
> *for they will be shown mercy.*
> *Blessed are the pure in heart,*
> *for they will see God.*

—MATTHEW 5:7-8

Of all the people who have ever lived, Jesus certainly had reason to let bitterness harden in his heart. He was constantly scorned and rejected, and lived His entire life knowing that He was destined for a terrible death on the cross. Yet He never gave in to bitterness. We find our way to Him through that same gentleness of spirit.

So the next time that you go through a major transition, try to focus on God's provision and care rather than the ways you think you've been let down. You can trust God's plans for you, and you can trust the people who care about you. God isn't out to get you just because something went wrong. In fact, He could be working in that misfortune to create an even more beautiful good! Even though it is difficult sometimes, we need to keep reminding ourselves of this important truth. "If your eyes are going to be on God," Jason said, "you need to take care of your heart. It needs to be soft."

To review, here are a few of the principles we went through in this chapter:

✝ Take time to fully understand how a change will affect you

✝ Focus on the big picture rather than the little changes

✝ Understand that God wants to use your doubts and struggles

✝ Find ways to talk about your doubts

✝ Set a positive, Godly example for others

✝ Don't allow bitterness to get between you and God

Chapter 12

ON THE REBOUND

Even if you do everything right, wholeheartedly embracing the Biblical principles we've outlined here, situations won't always turn out the way that you expect. Financial problems can be especially volatile. It's incredibly difficult to exactly predict the future of the market, the new challenges that may arise, or the other ways in which your personal or organisational finances could change unexpectedly.

So what do you do when disaster strikes? How should a Christian leader cope with challenging circumstances? Is it possible to maintain your vision and Godly character in the midst of financial turmoil?

Dr. William Frempong and Todd Gongwer are intimately acquainted with many kinds of difficult financial situations. When I spoke with these two men, they both shared stories of times when their faith in God was challenged as a result of financial turmoil. But they also shared stories of incredible success and encouragement, and I'd like to pass some of those stories on to you.

Dr. William Okyere Frempong is a medical doctor who is currently serv-ing as the Acting Medical Director of the LEKMA Polyclinic, a prominent government-sponsored health care facility just outside Accra, Ghana. He has spent his career in private practice, and dreams of establishing a health care system where each individual provider is empowered to work toward a compassionate, competent practice.

Outside of the medical world, Dr. Frempong is also the county director of the HuD Medical Consult, where he works as an administrator. In his time with HuD, Dr. Frempong also mentors other influential health care experts and trains them to promote healthy living in their communities.

Todd Gongwer has had a long career as an athlete, entrepreneur, and communicator. During the 1990s, Todd coached basketball at the national intercollegiate level. In later years, he wrote the popular "Need To Lead" development program, which has helped to revolutionise the leadership structures of many businesses and athletic teams.

Using the principles described in his book *Learn … For God's Sake!* Todd has spoken to athletic teams, non-profit organisations, and businesses all over the United States on topics related to leadership. Todd's ultimate goal is to help others discover their own purposes and passions.

With help from these two exceptional leaders, I've put together a list of principles to help encourage and advise you in the wake of a financial disaster. Hopefully, these principles will give you the same kind of hope they've given me.

PRINCIPLE #1: *YOU'RE MORE THAN YOUR MISTAKES*

After a few big failures early in life, Dr. Frempong learned to not place all of his trust in his own abilities. If you think of your work as a leader in terms of your own personal successes and failures, then you'll burn out when hard circumstances come around. Instead, think about your leadership work as an extension of God's work on earth.

Fixing his thoughts on God's purposes rather than his own doubts was what helped Dr. Frempong readjust his perspective after major disasters. "This is not me doing this," he shared. "I'm not here because I'm brilliant, or because I'm clever, or because I have what it takes. I'm here because God brought me here."

Your responsibility as a Christian leader is to pursue heavenly goals, not personal ambitions. Your story is larger than your own accomplishments and failures—it's a part of God's plan for the whole world. He is working in you, in the same way that He works in the world. So you don't need to be perfect all the time.

Understand that mistakes and misfortunes are part of the journey God has planned for you. Embrace them for what they are, and try to do as Dr. Frempong so wisely shared: "God puts us here to learn, to be refined and shaped. Our egos shouldn't get in the way of greater impact."

If you are focused on God's purposes rather than your own, then your view of failures will change. Instead of seeing setbacks as reflections on your own personal worth and skills, you can begin to view them as ways for God to show His provision for you. "When it's about Him," Dr. Frempong said, "then He will bring what you need."

PRINCIPLE #2: *YOU'RE HERE TO LEARN*

Much of Dr. Frempong's work with the HuD Group involves organising major medical conferences where local practitioners are trained in
public health initiatives. It was during one of these conferences that Dr.
Frempong's faith was tested.

"One of my first assignments was to execute a conference. We had sunk
a lot of money into it," he shared. "For me, this had been a big step of
faith. I had put in a lot of work, and I thought I had done all that needed
to be done. And the long and short of it was … it was a big flop! We
made huge losses."

Devastated by this disaster, Dr. Frempong spoke with a senior member
of the organisation for advice. What this fellow leader told him changed
his whole outlook: "One of the things that he shared with me, when I
lamented how disappointed I was, was this: 'Sometimes you win, and
sometimes you learn. So instead of feeling like a failure, gather the
lessons and use them in your planning.'"

This graciously-offered wisdom helped Dr. Frempong embrace a healthier attitude about the events that had occurred. He began to view this
unfortunate situation not as an abject failure, but as an immense opportunity for growth. "I realised that if I had executed this conference well,
and everything had gone to plan, then I might not have been quite so
careful the next time about all the things that needed to be done." The
next time your financial plans don't work out, spend some time reflecting
on what lessons you can learn from the experience.

PRINCIPLE #3: *YOU'RE NOT AN IMPOSTER*

Have you ever wondered if you only reached your position of leadership because of luck? Ever felt that you didn't deserve any of the successes or accolades that you've received? Ever looked at the people around you and thinking that some of them might actually be more qualified for your position than you are?

If so, then you're not alone! Many exemplary leaders have fallen prey to these doubts, which are often called "the Imposter Syndrome." In fact, these kinds of thoughts are incredibly common, even among people who are global leaders in their fields. So whether or not you're familiar with the terminology, you've probably experienced this mental phenomenon at some point in your leadership career.

When things go wrong, it's easy to doubt whether you're qualified to perform in your current role. Dr. Frempong is no stranger to these kinds of thoughts, but he's developed a wise philosophy for dealing with them. When he was asked to lead the LEKMA Polyclinic, he immediately began to doubt his ability to oversee such a massive operation.

But rather than dwelling on his misgivings, Dr. Frempong chose to focus on how many of his past experiences had prepared him to take on greater challenges. He firmly believes that all these experiences in his earlier career were part of God's plan for him and for the clinic. "Everything that happens in our lives is a preparation for some greater responsibility," he said.

Dr. Frempong also drew strength from his identity in Christ. "It's not who I am," he says, "but *whose* I am that matters." When you start to doubt your qualifications or abilities, think about the One who has prepared you for your leadership position. He knows what He's doing!

PRINCIPLE #4: *YOU'RE CHOSEN BY GOD*

In the middle of one normal day, Todd Gongwer had a catastrophic realisation: his life wasn't what he wanted to it to be, and he wasn't sure how to fix it. "It was a crash-and-burn time in my life," he said. "Nothing that I thought I had wanted to accomplish at this point in life had actually become what I thought it was going to become. I was financially—and emotionally—ruined."

A number of crises, many of them financial in nature, had combined to cause Todd a great amount of stress and doubt. "I found myself going back to that why question, asking myself 'Why am I doing what I'm doing?' and 'What am I doing on Earth?' I was trying to put the right label on things."

One moment stands out to Todd as a turning point in this difficult period. "There was a time when I was on my knees really struggling, and calling out to God, and my son walked through the door. For me, this was a really quick answer that I'd been looking for. God just opened my eyes." Todd shared that God showed him his true purpose on Earth in that moment: not to build up a fortune or a huge list of accomplishments, but to raise his family well and do God's work in the world.

Financial problems give us perspective. They help us to realise which things in life are genuinely important—such as our families, friendships, and spiritual callings—and which ones are not. Money is a means, not an objective. Our goal as Christian leaders, whether in business or ministry, should always be to steward our resources with wisdom rather than simply accumulate as much wealth as possible.

"It opens your mind to things that you once knew, or had in the back of your mind," Todd shared. "It helps you discover which things you aren't taking seriously enough."

In fact, Todd's spiritual life was revolutionised as a result of this very dark time. He stopped asking God to fulfil his every need, and started listening to God's voice instead. He began to value the other people in his life on their own terms, rather than his own. He started to notice the small moments in life that have eternal significance, rather than getting caught up in the daily grind.

Is God using difficult financial circumstances to get your attention? Maybe the challenges that you're facing are a sign that your priorities are in the wrong places. When times get tough, remember that money is not the most important thing in life. It comes and it goes. Other things, like our character and our relationship with God and others, will remain forever.

As a review, here are some of the truths we discussed in this chapter:

✞ Focus on God's plans rather than your own ambitions

✞ Look to your past experiences for confidence

✞ See mistakes or problems as learning experiences

✞ Find your identity in Christ, not in your accomplishments or failures

Sometimes our biggest enemy isn't outright failure, but burnout. Burnout is a familiar situation to anyone who's ever held a position of leadership. It can occur at the worst of times, and robs us of our confidence when we need it the most. We get bogged down in difficult questions like "If this is God's plan for me, then why am I so miserable?" or "Is this really what I'm supposed to be doing with my life?"

Nothing is more demoralising than a serious burnout. It can rob us of our confidence in God and in our own life work, our passion for the Kingdom, and our motivation to get things done. If you want to be an effective leader in your business or ministry, you must know how to avoid burnout and how to cope if it begins to affect you. The key to maintaining our confidence is to understand that burnout stems not from God's plan for us, but from an improper approach to carrying out those plans. We can maintain confidence in Him if we modify our attitudes and habits.

Thankfully, there are plenty of leaders in the world today who have learned how to handle burnout in their own lives and are willing to share that knowledge with us. If you want to conquer burnout in your own leadership journey, then you need to get both your mind and your heart in the right place. That means not only acquiring proactive strategies for defeating burnout when you see it in your life, but also cultivating a Godly mindset that prevents us from reaching that burnout stage in the first place. We need to treat the disease—not just its symptoms!

No one understands the intricacies of burnout quite like Scott Couchenour. Early in life, Scott made a successful career as the CEO of a prominent, national family business. As a result of the massive credit crunch of 2008, Scott's business suffered and eventually closed up shop. This difficult experience taught Scott many lessons about being an effective leader, motivating others, and keeping a whole team focused on a difficult goal.

After leaving his corporate position, Scott fell in love with life and business coaching. Today, as a certified small business coach, Scott helps leaders conquer irrelevance and burnout. His ultimate goal is to aid others in understanding their own organisational weaknesses, and to help them prevent those weaknesses from becoming serious problems down the road.

Working primarily with ministry leaders and small business owners, Scott uses a comprehensive analysis to discover the strengths and weaknesses of each organisation. When I spoke with Scott on the Podcast he had a lot of helpful advice for Christian leaders or entrepreneurs.

PRINCIPLE #1: SLOW DOWN!

The absolute first step to take when you find yourself confronted with burnout is to step back and reevaluate the pace of your life. Are you moving ahead so quickly that you aren't stopping to evaluate your life and work?

What is Scott's advice to leaders who feel like they're stuck in a cycle of stress and anxiety? "Slow down! God's never in a hurry." Scott remembers a life-changing piece of advice that he once received from his pastor: "He said to me 'Has it ever occurred to you that nothing has ever occurred to God?' He knows everything He's doing. After I heard that, I ceased all of the pressure I was putting on my mind." God works at His own pace—not society's pace, not the market's pace, and certainly not our pace!

Oftentimes, we get burnt out and stressed because we're referring to our own timeline rather than God's timeline. In our modern society, we think that we have to always pursue our goals aggressively—because who knows if the same opportunity will be there tomorrow? What we fail to remember is that the only opportunity that matters is the one that God has planned for us. Check out these verses from the gospel of Luke:

> *When all the people were being baptised, Jesus was baptised too. And as he was praying, heaven was opened, and the Holy Spirit descended on him in body form like a dove. And a voice came from heaven: 'You are my Son, whom I love; with you I am well pleased.' Now Jesus himself was about thirty years old when he began his ministry.*
>
> —LUKE 3:21-23, NIV

Jesus' ministry was the most effective and powerful influence that one person has ever had on the world, yet He didn't even begin to teach until an age when most of us have been established in our careers for several years. If God called us to wait to begin your work until you were thirty, or forty, or even fifty, many of us simply wouldn't have the patience or trust to wait on His timing.

Why did Jesus choose to wait for this long? Because He was operating according to God's schedule, not His own. Jesus knew that rushing God is never a good idea, because God orchestrates the circumstances around you in order to help you succeed. If God's plan is for you to become a full-time pastor or to assume leadership of your business, then He will bring those things about. It may take longer than we want it to, but this is only because God knows about many more variables than we do. What we need to do is watch and wait patiently for those opportunities to present themselves. And they will, in time—because, unlike our plans, God's plans never fail.

"I learned that instead of trying to manufacture things and make things happen, to allow Him to unfold things," Scott said. "Not just let Him do it, but do what I feel is right and let Him guide it." Waiting for God's timing certainly doesn't mean that we should just forget about doing His work in the world! After all, as Scott says: "You can't steer a car unless it's moving." Rather, we should yield to Him.

PRINCIPLE #2: DON'T JUST ASK—LISTEN!

When he feels stressed out and exhausted, Scott likes to practice something that he calls "listening prayer." This form of meditative prayer refreshes and empowers. Most importantly, it helps to renew our confidence in God's plans.

How does it work? "Listening prayer is deceptively simple," Scott said. "Think of it like lying back on the bank of a river and not forcing your thoughts, but simply being there to listen to God in silence. No praying, no 'Dear God, help me do this.' And as a thought comes down the river, let it keep going. Just listen."

The important thing to remember when practicing a "listening" prayer is to not focus on an objective: don't think about what you want God to give you, or about how you want Him to help you out, or about all the stressful things you need to accomplish today. It's focusing too much on those kinds of end goals that usually makes us burnt out in the first place! Many of us allow the mindset that we apply to work—where our focus is on getting things done—to characterise our relationship with God as well. But God is not a tool that we use to accomplish our goals. He's a loving Father who wants to nurture us emotionally and motivate us spiritually. Our relationship with God should be something that refreshes us and reminds us of His powerful love for us.

Even Jesus had to take the time to listen and reconnect with His Father. There are many moments where the Bible tells us he withdrew to talk to God in private. During these times, He always made sure that He was alone, in a quiet place, and not distracted by the worries of the day. Take this passage from Mark as an example:

> *Very early in the morning, while it was still dark,*
> *Jesus got up, left the house, and went off to a solitary place,*
> *where he prayed.*

> *—Mark 1:35, NIV*

Phrases like this are very common throughout the gospels, simply because Christ understood stress and tiredness as well as anyone who has ever lived. After all, it would probably be very tiring to have hundreds of people following you around asking for miracles all the time! If listening prayer was good enough for Jesus when He was on Earth, then it's more than sufficient to deal with our busy modern lives.

So why not make listening prayer a part of your daily routine? Allow prayer to be enjoyable and restful again. Listening prayer is a fantastic discipline to keep up all the time, but it's especially important when we're tired and stressed out. Taking time out of your day to rest and rejuvenate in God's presence will remind you of His presence and care, which in turn will renew your confidence in His plans for you.

Importantly, Scott notes that God doesn't always answer us during these times of listening prayer. But if we continually approach Him in this humble, "In the process of consistently praying," he said, "I was able to realise that the more frequently I quieted myself before God, the more He was able to speak to me. It wasn't anything that He had to change. I had to become receptive." If you recharge every day with meditative prayer, you'll notice this pattern of being receptive.

PRINCIPLE #3: *REEVALUATE YOUR PRIORITIES*

Of course, preventing burnout long-term usually means a complete revolution of your attitude. Severe burnout happens because we make a habit of stretching ourselves too thin and trying to do too many things. What's the solution? Rearranging our priorities!

The first thing to do is to determine which things bring you the most purpose and fulfilment. Maybe, for you, that thing is charting a long-term course for your business or leading a ministry at your church. It certainly doesn't need to fit with society's idea of accomplishment. "Success is not being a CEO!" Scott said. "Success is realising what you are really good at and being able to operate within that 80% of your waking hours. Some percentage of our life will be things that we don't like to do. But for me, success is working in my wheelhouse and being willing to pivot on the direction of the Spirit." Though every leadership position entails some tasks you won't enjoy, you should be fulfilled in your calling. This should be your barometer of success, and should determine how you arrange the rest of your priorities.

Scott believes that each of us has the power to live a stress-free, happy life, if we apply ourselves wisely. The key is to not allow ourselves to be overwhelmed by the deluge of information that we experience every day. As Scott commented: "The problem is not with a lack of information, but lack of implementation. We have so much information coming at us that we don't know how to take what we need and make it a sustainable change in our lives." In order to make a substantial, lasting change in our lives, we need to take time to pause, reflect and focus on the things that really matter.

Scott likes to approach his weekly schedule through the idea of what he calls "the 1-7 dream." As he describes the concept: "What's the one thing you can do over the next seven days that will get you closer to your dream?" Once you've figured out that one crucial component, then bump it up to the top of your to-do list. That's the most important thing you need to do this week!

You also need to figure out which tasks *aren't* as important, which sometimes means giving up on ideas and projects you're very passionate about. "I've learned that just because I have an idea, it's not a good reason to jump off a cliff and do it," Scott says. "I've learned to put it in a 'waiting room,' to put it away and revisit it. If it keeps recurring, it's something worth pursuing." If that fantastic plan doesn't occur to you more than once, however, then it's probably not a calling from the Lord. Set it aside.

This kind of self-examination will keep you from loading yourself down with obligations and projects that aren't truly part of God's calling for you. All great leaders have powerful ideas, but you are only one person and there are only so many hours in a day! As leaders, we need to leverage our time for the biggest possible impact. That means saying no to some things that seem beneficial and not getting distracted by other opportunities.

Armed with this new knowledge about your priorities, Scott finds it helpful to approach each week with a concrete schedule in mind. "If I don't have a reoccurring list of things that I do daily—every Monday, Tuesday, and so on—then I get lost," he said. "I could go in fifty different directions. I used to go home overwhelmed and further behind than I started the day. It's a matter of expectations. That list keeps me focused. I learned that if I can go into every day with three things to get done in the day, then I've got enough time to get those three. If I get all three done, I can borrow from tomorrow's three."

Setting up boundaries and guidelines like this is a very Biblical concept. If we closely examine Jesus' ministry throughout the gospels, we see a man who knew his limits and set up boundaries. We like to think of Christ as a person who was always available to others, but there are many times in the gospels when He refused to heal the sick or teach because He needed to spend time with God or rest. That doesn't mean that Jesus didn't care about other people—in fact, it's just the opposite! Christ cared enough for others to give them His best, which often means knowing where to draw boundaries and keep yourself healthy. Then, whenever other people need your help, you can give them attention that isn't divided by exhaustion and worry. Godly leaders know that they need to rest in order to give others their best.

PRINCIPLE #4: *FIND A CREATIVE CONNECTION*

What about strategies for preventing burnout in the long term? Many leaders find that one of the most effective ways to ward off burnout is to find some sort of creative outlet to share their frustrations and successes with others who might be in similar situations.

Scott found that release in sharing his thoughts online. "For me, the outlet was blogging," he said. "In my blogging, I was careful to ask myself: 'Am I being truthful? Am I being authentic?' I found that through the course of typing onto my keyboard—not things like 'I'm perfect, here's what you should be doing!'—I shared things like, 'This is what I'm struggling with. Does anybody else struggle with it?' Just be yourself, and be real. If you take that jump, you will realise that you're drawing people to you when you're authentic."

Finding a platform to share your story—whether through writing or some other form of creative expression—is key to building a stress-free life. It allows you to vent your frustrations, share with others, and release your emotions in a healthy way instead of letting them build up inside. As a leader, you owe it to others to give them your very best self.

As a review, here are the burnout-conquering strategies we've covered in this chapter:

✟ Slow down and pay attention to God's timeline

✟ Spend time each day in meditative prayer

✟ Figure out your biggest priorities, and don't waste time on the other things

✟ Write a schedule for your week—and stick to it!

✟ Find a creative way to share your passions and frustrations with others

Chapter 14 | OVERCOMING INSTITUTIONAL PREJUDICE

Godly leadership can be a difficult enough challenge without having to contend with the biases and prejudices of others. However, many leaders find that there are obstacles in their path that they cannot con-trol. Some of the greatest leaders are those who have overcome great prejudices. Issues like gender and race are sadly still very prevalent and controversial in the marketplace and in many ministries. How should we, as Christian leaders, handle these situations in a compassionate and mature manner without compromising our mission?

In this final chapter, we'll be hearing from several women who have done groundbreaking, revolutionary work in their churches and communities. These women fought to overcome years of tradition, the negative opin-ions of others in order to do what God was calling them to do in the world. Though they have mainly shared their experiences as women in ministry, the lessons they have learned are broadly applicable to anyone who wants to overcome this kind of institutional prejudice.

Hopefully these women's examples of grace and wisdom will be as great an encouragement to you as they were to me!

DR. A'NDREA WILSON: *OPEN YOUR MIND*

A lifelong book lover and the author of the popular *Wife 101* novel series, Dr. D'Andrea Wilson is also well regarded for her work in the field of psychology. With degrees in marriage and family counselling as well as educational leadership, Dr. Wilson specialises in fiction that examines marriage and relationship issues with the benefit of a clinical psychological background. She's also the president and founder of Divine Garden Press, an independent publisher that specialises in high-quality, inspirational Christian fiction.

"One of the things that God has made me is a truth-teller," Dr. Wilson said. "I think it's important, as a writer, to not be ashamed of the Gospel." Though her tendency to be blunt about her opinions has sometimes gotten her into trouble, it's also turned out to be a huge asset in her career as a fiction writer. Trusting in God also means trusting in the unique abilities He's given you, even if you don't understand their worth. It's easy to see your personality as a liability, especially when others are overly critical, but God's calling and approval is more important than the world's.

"Just be yourself," Dr. Wilson said. "We definitely live in a world that wants to change you, to make you what they think is great. The world will pick you apart, find areas that they think are flaws, and rob you of your sense of confidence to believe that you can be all God has called you to be." Rather than be discouraged by others' criticisms, remain resolute and focused on what you believe it is that God has called you to do and trust that He will guide you through.

"One of the things that God has made me is a truth-teller," she said. "I think it's important, as a writer, to not be ashamed of the Gospel." Though her tendency to be blunt about her opinions has sometimes gotten her into trouble, it's also turned out to be a huge asset in her career as a fiction writer. Trusting in God also means trusting in the unique abilities He's given you, even if you don't understand their worth. Remember that His strength is made perfect in our weakness!

REVEREND KATE COLEMAN: ACCEPT THE CALL

Reverend Kate Coleman is a prominent lecturer, public speaker, and mentor, who is internationally known for her work in church leadership. She was the first black woman to assume leadership in a U.K. Baptist church. Her book, *Seven Deadly Sins of Women in Leadership,* has helped many other women in ministry understand their unique role as spiritual pioneers. Most of her time is spent meeting with leaders from various businesses, charities, and ministries, and instructing them in leadership principles.

Reverend Coleman remembers very clearly the time when she first heard God's call, during a spiritual retreat on top of a mountain. "I was there for three weeks, fasting and praying," she shared. "In that time, God spoke very clearly and said 'I've called you to lead, I've called you to shepherd my people.' It was a real shock, because—obviously—I'm a woman, in a particular church that didn't believe in women's leadership. And neither did I! But I was hearing God calling me into leadership, but at the same time struggling with how that could be possible."

Sometimes it's very important to have some time alone, so as to shut out other people's discouragements and focus instead on what God is saying to you. When we are surrounded by negative views of our own worth, we can lose sight of His call on our lives. So be sure to take time on your own, like Rev. Coleman did, to discern God's voice from the crowd.

It's also important to open up an honest dialogue with God about His plans for you, especially if those plans involve going against social expectations. You'll probably be feeling unsure of your own abilities or even frustrated with God for asking you to do something so far outside your comfort zone. That's all perfectly normal. The wise thing to do is to go to God in prayer and ask Him to show you His will.

As Rev. Coleman remembers: "I said to God: 'This doesn't make sense to me, so if it's You, then You'll have to make this happen.' I didn't tell anybody else about it immediately—but within two years of that I was leading my church!" As it happens, the overseers of Rev. Coleman's church had also been convicted about their own attitudes toward women in leadership, and they wanted to show their support by appointing her one of the church's new elders. This decision caused a lot of scandal and division in Rev. Coleman's congregation at the time, but the support and shared calling of the church overseers helped Rev. Coleman to see past the struggles.

This story just goes to show that you never know exactly what work God is bringing about in the hearts and minds of the people around you. Rev. Coleman couldn't see how her call could possibly fit into the culture she was a part of, but that was only because she didn't know that God was changing the overseer's hearts as well as her own. Though Rev. Coleman didn't see herself as a pioneer at that time, she looks back and sees how God was using her to pave new roads for women in other Baptist churches. "You don't have the luxury to say no," Rev. Coleman said. "I need to not just look back and recognise that I'm breaking new ground, but I need to now be intentional about breaking new ground." If you have been given the opportunity to pave the way for others in your organisation or business, then seize it! Remember that you don't just accept the call once in your life: you must continue to speak to God about the struggles and passions He places on your life.

"For me, success is about faithfulness to the call, not numbers or figures," Rev. Coleman said. "I always use the comparison between Moses and Jesus: Moses leads over two million people in the desert. Most people don't have a church organisation that size, so they'll think that is a success. But Jesus comes down from Heaven and leads twelve people—and He changes the world! So success is faithfulness to what I believe God's asking me to do, in the face of what may appear to be failure in the eyes of others."

DR. ESI ANSAH: BE BIGGER

A dedicated academic and internationally sought leadership coach, Dr. Esi Ansah is also a founding partner and CEO of Axis Human Capital, which aims to change the way people work in her native Ghana. She also works with the Association of Ghana's Elders, where she works to record the life stories and leadership lessons from prominent senior citizens in her community, as well as an assistant professor of leadership and human resources. She spends her time teaching, working with young people, and speaking all over the world on topics as diverse as policy reform, leadership theory, and education.

Dr. Ansah comes from a family of academics, and has always been a teacher at heart. Laughing, she remembered pulling neighbourhood children aside and "forcing" them to let her help them with their homework! Over time, she realised that those gifts and talents could be put to use in the academic world, and she's discovered that some of her toughest opposition comes from authority figures who refuse to acknowledge her achievements because of her gender or age. "For me, it's difficult being put in situations where I'm leading people older than myself," Dr. Ansah shared. "The challenge there is in finding that fine line between deferring to them and making a case that they may not favour. It's always been a challenge, but God gives us wisdom in our time of need."

How does Dr. Ansah navigate the difficult waters of organisational conflict? "Be nice, and polite," she says, "but still manage to get things done even if they don't particularly like it. See the point of view of others without shutting them down." Expect some pettiness and stubbornness from others, but never stoop to that level yourself.

Dr. Ansah particularly recommends contacting others in private to discuss controversial issues. "Say to them, 'I understand what you're saying and I understand you want to go in this direction, but it's really essential because of your influence that you're more careful. What about if we do it this way? Do you think this could work?' Get them to begin reasoning. Then come back to the group." Approaching people individually allows you to build relationships with them, listen to their perspective, and exchange ideas outside of the conflict you may be experiencing. A great leader values both cooperation and productivity, and has honest conversations with those who oppose them.

REVEREND EVE PITTS: KNOW YOURSELF

Rev. Canon Eve Pitts is an energetic, passionate leader whose sermons are internationally regarded for their humour, authenticity, and courage. She was the first black woman to be ordained in the Church of England, and has continued to blaze trails for women in ministry ever since.

During my discussion with Rev. Pitts, she shared that she initially struggled with the pressure to conform to what others wanted her to be. She said: "I said to God, 'If I'm going to be a leader in the church, I have to be myself. Please don't call me into any church where I can't be who

I am. I will learn to deal with the things that are not good and creative and healthy for me, but I don't want to be in a position where I have to pretend to be something else. I want the church to accept me as I am, with all the idiosyncrasies I possess!" Many of us—even those with strong personalities—feel the pressure to conform to our environments. This temptation is especially strong when we feel like an outsider. But we must remember that we are uniquely shaped by God for a purpose. You're greatest fulfilment will come from being yourself.

As Rev. Pitts said: "If you stop learning about who you are, then you become a danger to the souls of others. You have to be acutely aware of your own failures. I'm very suspicious of ministers who cannot be critical of themselves." She believes that self-knowledge and acceptance are the first steps to confidence in God's plans, particularly when that acceptance isn't forthcoming from others. In order to be an effective and Godly leader, you must understand where you're liable to make mistakes and where you are likely to succeed. In this way, you'll be able to take an appropriate amount of pride in your achievements, and won't be caught off guard by others' criticisms when they come.

Thankfully, this process of self-knowledge doesn't need to be totally complete before you can start living out God's plan for you. Rather, it's a process that stays with you for your entire leadership journey. "I'm at a place now where I'm fascinated with myself, because I still feel as if I've just started ministry," Rev. Pitts shared. "I continue to learn about my response to people, how I perceive them, how I acknowledge that they're different from myself. It behooves a leader to remember that the people you meet are on their own journey. I'm still excited about learning to love the people I meet, even when it's very difficult." Rev. Pitts stays excited about her calling and her abilities, which helps her stay grounded when opposition comes.

What do all of these women have in common? For one, they all have extremely open and honest relationships with God. It's particularly important to foster that bond with your Father when you're facing prejudice from other people. They also unabashedly embrace their unique strengths, acknowledge their weaknesses, and understand how to relate to opponents with grace and humility.

Here are some of the practical ways that you can tackle prejudice in your workplace or ministry:

✝ Foster pride in your accomplishments, and don't let others' negativity steal your joy

✝ Spend time alone with God to discern His voice from the crowd

✝ Always practice politeness and discretion in your interactions with those who critique you

✝ Be aware of your own strengths and weaknesses, and never stop learning new things

The ability to focus on key activities and delegate or eliminate the rest

Chapter 15

PRESERVING AND PROTECTING TRUST

Trust is absolutely essential to the relationship between a leader and their team. Whenever this trust is broken it greatly affects the cohesive-ness of the group, which in turn can have devastating consequences in the long term.

One man who's certainly seen a great deal of "people problems" is Dr. John Andrews. John has worked in various areas of church admin-istration and ministry for almost 20 years, and is passionate about empowering other church leaders to live like Christ. During his career, he has planted a church in West Yorkshire, repurposed the Hub Christian Community in South Yorkshire, and served as Senior Associate Leader of the Renewal Christian Centre in Solihull, an innovative and out-reach-focused Christian community.

John now serves as the Principal of the British Assemblies of God Bible College, where he loves helping to equip the next generation of servant leaders. Through the years he has also authored eleven books, such as *Moving Beyond Mediocrity* and *The Freedom of Limitation—Going Beyond By Staying Within.*

As evidenced by this long list of accomplishments, John is a driven, purposeful leader who brings huge dreams and a powerful energy to all of his projects. More importantly, all of John's projects have required him to build and maintain relationships with other people. John's many years of leadership experience in the church have given him a wealth of practical knowledge about how to handle tough personal conflicts and keep teams together even when things go wrong.

Every interpersonal conflict will be different. Despite their complicated nature, however, there are still a number of valuable lessons that can help leaders avoid and resolve these issues when they occur. John shared several of these leadership lessons with me, and in the next few sections I'd like to pass a few of them on to you.

LESSON #1: BE CONFIDENT IN YOURSELF

Here's a step that you can take on your own, before any personal conflicts have the chance to appear. This may seem contradictory, but the first step to maintaining a trusting relationship with others is to be confident in your own abilities. If you don't trust yourself to lead your team competently and effectively, then it can be harder for them to trust your leadership. It's difficult for a team of people to take directions from someone who doesn't believe that their dreams or ideas have value.

There may not be an easy formula for becoming more confident, but a true leader's self-confidence comes from relying on God's strength. Let go of any fears you might have of not being smart enough for your job, of not being a good enough speaker or writer, or of not being a "natural leader." After all, God has brought you into your leadership position, and God's power is sufficient to do anything that He has called you to do!

Look to the example of John the Baptist, a man whose whole purpose was to lead people to Christ. When he was questioned about his purposes, he replied: "He [God] must become greater and greater; I must become less." John understood that it wasn't about his ability, but rather his availability.

So if you ever find yourself doubting your leadership abilities, try to remember that your purpose is to call attention to God, and not yourself. Trust that He will give you all of the tools you need to do your job well. If your team sees that you fully trust God's purposes, it will be easier for them to fully trust your plans.

LESSON #2: SET REALISTIC GOALS

When I spoke to John he shared this lesson, which he has learned through many interpersonal disappointments and conflicts. One very important strategy you can use to avoid broken trust is to always set realistic goals for the people under your leadership.

John shared that while setting ambitious goals is very important, it isn't worth sacrificing the unity of his team. What's important to him is "realising that the people you are leading or the people in your team are also processing a journey." Great church and business leaders understand that not everyone on their team is in the same stage of that personal journey.

This lesson can be difficult to learn, especially for leaders—like John— who have a great deal of individual passion and ambition. In fact, this has been one of John's greatest challenges as he tries to interact graciously and effectively with the members of his team. Part of this is because he holds such strong personal convictions about his purposes. "I'm passionate about high standards for myself," he shared with me. "Because of that, I sort of expect everybody else to be the same."

But the fact is that not everyone on your team will have exactly the same priorities as you. Some of them won't have the same sense of urgency or passion that you probably feel about all your projects. Beyond this, not everyone works at the same pace or has the same abilities as you or the most productive members of your team might have.

However, this doesn't necessarily mean that someone isn't a "team player" or doesn't contribute anything to the group: it is merely a reflection of the Biblical principle that different people have different talents and gifts. Nevertheless, this disparity between people's abilities can sometimes create tension. Those who move quickly are disappointed by others' slower pace, and those who aren't quite as driven often feel left behind or undervalued.

How can we work to avoid this issue in our own organisations? John recommends making your team's empowerment a top priority, rather than focusing solely on getting as much done as quickly as possible. It is your job as the leader to ensure that everyone feels comfortable, understands what is required of them and that they have the tools and resources to be able to get their job done in the agreed timeframe.

Make it a policy to only give your team assignments that you know they will be able to complete within the time frame you've given them and to the quality that you expect. Don't ask your team to pull together a huge project at the last minute. And always be sure to give a complete, clear explanation of the expectations that you have for everyone before the work even gets off the ground.

It's certainly a good thing to challenge people, but never make requests that go beyond their capabilities or resources. That is the easiest way to ruin the bond of trust that you have with the members of your team.

Ask yourself questions like:

✞ "Have I given everyone the information and resources they need to complete this job?"

✞ "Have I set a deadline that's possible to accomplish?"

✞ "Have I delegated responsibilities to people according to their talents and abilities?"

✞ Taking advantage of this short process of reflection early in every project will help to avoid plenty of confusions and possible conflicts later on.

LESSON #3: EXTEND FORGIVENESS

Of course, no matter how careful we are in our demands, any group of people will experience some degree of interpersonal conflict at some point in its development. That's just how people are.

It's best to be prepared for this scenario ahead of time: understand that every great leader has had to deal with "people problems" at one time or another. In fact, it's their ability to behave with compassion and understanding in a conflict that separates the good leaders from the great ones.

The next element of dealing with broken relationships or trust is a fundamental Christian principle that nonetheless applies in any situation, either in the ministry or the marketplace. It's a simple action that can still be very difficult to learn: forgiveness. Forgiveness doesn't just mean forgetting that anything bad happened—it's an intentional effort to mend any wounds that have been created.

As an illustration, imagine this scenario: someone in your business or church team didn't show up to a very important meeting. Perhaps the person who the missing team member was supposed to collaborate with feels rejected. Other people in the group are exasperated by this team member's apparent lack of dedication to the group. And you, as the leader, are probably feeling very disappointed or even angry that one person could let the rest of you down in this way, particularly if it was a project that was very important to you.

Part of your role as a leader is to help everyone sort through these kinds of messy situations. The first thing to do is make an effort to understand the roots of the conflict: was it a simple misunderstanding, a foolish mistake, or a deliberate act of cruelty towards another person? Be sure to remain fair, and to listen to as many sides of the issue as you can.

After you've uncovered the source of the conflict, take some time to verbally acknowledge the different types of hurt that everyone in the team might be feeling at this time. Let everyone know that you understand their feelings and are working to find a solution.

Dealing with these kinds of issues sometimes requires making hard choices, but make sure that any action you take is motivated by reconciliation rather than vengeance. In fact, the Bible explicitly tells us to treat an offender in this way:

> *You ought to forgive and comfort him,*
> *so that he will not be overwhelmed by excessive sorrow.*

> —2 CORINTHIANS 2:7, NIV

Most importantly, let your team see you reaching out to the person who has broken their trust. It's your responsibility to model Jesus for them, and Jesus always forgave.

LESSON #4: DON'T GIVE IN TO BITTERNESS

Even if you do your best to prevent conflict and broken relationships within your team, chances are that you'll still find yourself confronted with some kind of difficult interpersonal situation during your time as a leader.

How do you cope when someone you rely on, either in your church or in your business, disappoints your or betrays your trust? One of the most important things to watch out for during these unfortunate situations is the growth of bitterness.

In the book of James in the Bible we can find some valuable insight into what happens when we allow bitterness to take hold of our hearts:

> But if you harbour bitter envy and selfish ambition in your hearts, do not boast about it or deny the truth. Such "wisdom" does not come down from heaven but is earthly, unspiritual, demonic. For where you have envy and selfish ambition, there you find disorder and every evil practice.

—JAMES 3:14-16, NIV

Why does bitterness exercise such a powerful negative influence on our hearts?

Most importantly, it hampers your ability to interact with your team in a Godly way. A person who clings to their anger and petty thoughts even after the conflict has been resolved is setting himself or herself up for failure in the long term.

The most crucial thing to do after an interpersonal conflict is to work on restoring your team's sense of unity and purpose. This can be a challenging task, and one that requires all of your mental and emotional strength. You won't be able to pull your team back together if you're too caught up in your own residual feelings about what happened, so make sure that you sort through your anger with prayer and reflection before you talk to the rest of the team.

Another important thing to remember is that as a leader, you are continuously setting an example for your team with your attitudes, words, and actions. If your team sees that you're still acting out of anger or harbouring bad feelings toward someone, they may feel that it's all right to do the same. So don't allow the pain you may feel to turn you away from your purposes—think of it as an opportunity to grow in Christ and show His love to others in a new way.

Remember that every team works at its best when all its members are comfortable depending on each other and trusting you to lead them well. Your primary goal should be repairing the bond of trust that holds your team together.

Sometimes the only way to do this is to let go of the people who've caused the conflict, especially if their behaviour hasn't changed for the better. At other times you might need to modify the way your organisation operates, or mediate a disagreement between team members.

Each individual situation will call for a different method, but the most important thing to remember is that your team will take their cue from your actions. So no matter what tough personal situations you might face, be sure to always set a Christlike example in your words and actions!

To review, here are some of the valuable leadership lessons that we've discussed in this chapter:

✝ Trust in God's purposes and provision

✝ Understand that not everyone on your team has the same capabilities

✝ Focus on empowering others

✝ Set reasonable expectations for your team

✝ Model Christlike forgiveness

✝ Don't allow pain to develop into bitterness

Chapter 16

IT'S NOT ABOUT YOU

At 15 years old, Jeffery Lestz discovered Jesus on the rough-and-tum-ble streets of Chicago. Jeffrey's life before his conversion had often been a tumultuous one: after growing up in a Jewish family, he was orphaned at a young age and spent his middle school years moving from foster home to foster home.

By the age of 19, Jeffrey had already entered the world of professional sales, and by working hard and being sensible with his finances he had already become a millionaire by his early thirties. During this journey Jeffrey developed a passion for what he calls the "mysteries of money," spiritual principles that can revolutionise the way we think about per-sonal wealth and financial stability.

Jeffrey loves sharing the lessons that the Bible can teach us about financial responsibility and a Christlike attitude toward money. His pas-sion is to fill the gaps that he sees in traditional financial education both by helping families become independent and debt free, and advising pastors about how to integrate Biblical stewardship principles into their ministry. Today, Jeff also serves on the Board of Directors at London Hillsong, which is also his home church.

During his career as a financial and ministry advisor, Jeffrey has brought hope and stability to a countless number of households. In addition, his many books—including *True Riches* and *Prosperity With Purpose*—have helped thousands of people discover the Biblical "mysteries of money" and apply them practically to their own lives.

What are some of the principles that helped to propel Jeffrey to business and ministry success? He shared several of them with me, and now I'd like to pass them on to you.

PRINCIPLE #1: *KNOW YOUR OWN ABILITIES*

It may feel paradoxical to begin a chapter titled "It's Not About You" with thinking about your own strengths and talents, but a leader who is aware of their own capabilities has laid a foundation for a strong, healthy team.

Whether you work in the marketplace or the ministry, you can likely identify some of the characteristics that have led you to your leadership position. Maybe you're an exceptionally good administrator, or are skilled in interpersonal communication, or are great at inspiring others to action. These are the qualities that God has given you to in order to equip you in your task of leading others.

So take a moment to jot down some of the areas that you consider to be your greatest strengths. Your list might look like this:

☦ Great at delegating tasks

☦ Compassionate and caring

☦ Has lots of financial knowledge

Once you have a solid list of strengths, spend some time thinking about how you can best use these gifts to encourage and support your team. Are you using them to your full potential?

If you really want to dig deeper and understand your team's potential even further, then dedicate a few more minutes to identifying some your weaknesses. These might be abilities or skills for which you may not have a natural aptitude, personal situations that may limit your work capabilities, or duties that you just don't particularly enjoy being responsible for. Not great at organisation? Bored by long meetings? Find it difficult to keep a schedule? Write it all down. Be honest with yourself!

This task can sometimes be a little bit discouraging, so it is important to keep in mind that having a list of weaknesses doesn't mean that you are not an effective or competent leader. Remember that God has given you a unique set of talents and abilities for a specific reason: to be the leader of your team. He has equipped you for the work that you are doing now, and will continue to enable you to succeed in your position as long as you remain dependent on His provision.

Being totally honest about your strengths and weaknesses will help you to stay humble and aware of your own limitations. Someone who has made a genuine appraisal of their strengths and is confident in God's personal provision will be much less likely to constantly seek the approval of others. And most importantly—a leader who has spent time reflecting on his or her own personal qualities will understand that they can't do it all on their own!

PRINCIPLE #2: *AVOID JEALOUSY*

Once you've established a list of what you're good at and what you're not so good at, you can move on to figuring out how that knowledge can shape the rest of your team.

Jeffrey Lestz is certainly a great example of a leader who is highly gifted and has a lot of personal ambition. He has faced a multitude of challenges, and his work in financial counselling has given him plenty of expertise in dealing with sensitive personal situations. During his many years involved in both business and ministry, Jeffrey has faced plenty of tough situations.

What does Jeffrey think of as the biggest challenge he's faced during his time as a leader? When I spoke with him, he had a surprising answer: "Realising how to utilise other people in their gifts, and not to be jealous with those gifts. Realising that I cannot be everybody."

God has given each member of your team their own sets of talents and weaknesses, and they are likely not the same as yours. If you think about it, this is actually a huge asset: great teams are able to compensate for each other's weaknesses with their own skills. Really, that's what being a team is all about!

This is where your list of strengths and weaknesses will become most useful. Look back over the things that you identified as weaknesses, then think about your team. For each weakness, ask yourself some focusing questions:

✝ Is there someone on the team who could do this job better?

✝ Do I feel comfortable handing this responsibility over to them?

✝ If not, why? Is it because I don't want to give up control over this responsibility?

If you're clinging to a responsibility that someone else might do better, maybe it's time to reevaluate your attitude.

Great leaders' downfall often lies in pride. When you've been given a prominent and influential position in your organisation, it can be tempting to think that you can—and should—do it all. Even though this is a spiritual issue, it doesn't just affect leaders in ministry; everyone "We let our egos get in the way," Jeffrey told me, especially if we are inexperienced or over-confident in our own abilities. "We think that we know better."

It's great to feel like you're in control of your team, but that never means that you have to take every responsibility onto your own shoulders. Learn to lean on others, and soon you'll find that their strengths are

PRINCIPLE #3: *TAKE ONE FOR THE TEAM*

When Jesus was sending his apostles out into the world to minister, he encouraged them with these powerful words not to be like worldly leaders:

> *Not so with you. Instead, whoever wants to become great among you must be your servant, and whoever wants to be first must be slave of all. For even the Son of Man did not come to be served, but to serve.*

—MARK 10:43-45A

That is a powerful statement! If Jesus, the Son of God, was willing to make great sacrifices for his disciples, then a truly Christlike leader will also make sure to put the needs of other members of the team far above his or her own.

Remember, his death on the cross wasn't the only sacrifice Jesus made. He also continuously sacrificed his time, his energy, and his comfort during his ministry. There are many times in the Bible when Jesus simply wanted to be alone and pray, but instead he went out to speak to the people or talk amongst the disciples. This is a great example of true servant leadership. Jesus knew that some things were more important than His personal preferences.

Almost anyone can bark out commands or put together a project, but it takes a great leader to make real sacrifices for his or her team. The secular world tells us that a leadership position is a great time to "get ahead" and But as Christian leaders, we are expected to go above and beyond the world's ideas of success, leading with selflessness and genuine humility.

See your influential position not as a way to promote your own inter-ests, but as an opportunity to exemplify Christian principles to a greater number of people and to help carry out God's plans for the people around you.

Sometimes sacrificial leadership might mean working late to help your team on a project when all you really want to do is go home and relax. Sometimes it might mean putting some personal funds toward a project that you'd rather have used to go on vacation.

Making these types of sacrifices will never be easy—it was even difficult for Jesus Himself! But in the long term, the personal rewards that you reap from these acts of sacrificial leadership will far outweigh any of the sacrifices that you've made.

PRINCIPLE #4: KEEP GOD FIRST

One of the traps that many leaders fall into is looking to other people for approval rather than trusting God's calling for their lives. Every leader has struggled with this temptation, but truly great leaders know to seek God first.

In fact, the apostle Paul opened his letter to the Galatians by introducing himself as sent *"not from men nor by a man, but by Jesus Christ and God the Father." (Galatians 1:1, NIV)* Here was an awesome leader who was clearly up-front about where he sought approval! Later in the letter, he makes an even more obvious statement about how true Godly leaders should think about fulfilment:

> *Am I now trying to win the approval of human beings,*
> *or of God? Or am I trying to please people? If I were still*
> *trying to please people, I would not be a servant of Christ.*

Clearly, Godly leadership is very different from the picture the world paints for us of how a leader should think, talk, and act. Where people who follow the world's idea of leadership think of themselves as the most important part of the picture, leaders like Paul understand that they are only instruments serving God's purposes in the world. God's approval is worth far more than the approval of others—rest in that knowledge

If, at any time in your leadership journey, you find that you're thinking more about your personal image than your team's wellbeing or God's purposes for you, it may be time to reevaluate your view of healthy leadership. Being a leader isn't about enjoying your influence or looking "cool." It's about using the gifts God has given you to positively influence your team, your business or ministry, and the whole world.

We are more susceptible to this kind of self-centered thinking at certain points in our leadership journeys: when we've just completed an important project, or when we've led our team through a challenging time, or even when we just feel very confident about the plans we've laid for the future.

This can happen to all leaders, regardless of whether you're serving as the lead pastor in a large church or an entrepreneur running a small start-up business. We are all human, but God's power is greater than our weaknesses. Keep your eyes fixed on His plans.

It's about Him—not about you!

To wrap up, here are some of the key concepts we've tackled in this chapter:

✝ Become familiar with your own strengths and weaknesses

✝ Remember that you don't need to "do it all"

✝ Don't be jealous of others' unique talents and gifts

✝ Be willing to make sacrifices for your team

✝ Always seek God's approval, rather than the approval of others

Chapter 17

THE VALUE OF AUTHENTIC
RELATIONSHIPS

When you strip away all the extraneous factors, getting to know people is really all about building relationships that have trust and authenticity. Great leaders thrive because they have a thorough understanding of how to create and maintain such relationships.

Brad Lomenick is someone who understands the true value of authen-tic Christian friendships. Before moving into his current position, he worked in the field of management consulting and helped to grow the popular Life@Work Magazine. Today, Brad is the Strategic Director of Catalyst, a ministry that focuses on inspiring and empowering the next generation of Christian leadership. He spends his time consult-ing with young ministry influencers, speaking at training events, and strengthening the global community of rising Christian leaders. Above all, Brad is passionate about personal growth, teamwork, social media outreach, and more, and he frequently addresses these topics in his books and consulting sessions. His books, *The Catalyst Leader* and *H3 Leadership,* aim to help young leaders understand their unique potential in the global church.

When I spoke with Brad, he really emphasised the value of authenticity in Christian relationships, especially the relationship between a leader and his team. He offered me a lot of practical advice about cultivating that authenticity in our lives. In the sections to follow, I'll outline some of the principles that Brad identified as crucial to Christian relationships, and explain some ways that you can cultivate these qualities in your own relationships.

PRINCIPLE #1: MUTUAL PURPOSE

There is no better foundation for a friendship than a shared faith in God's purposes and call on your lives. Think of some of the great friendships and working partnerships in the Bible: David and Jonathan, Ruth and Naomi, Paul and Timothy. All these people shared, life-giving, lifelong relationships with each other because they came from a shared commitment to God.

Plenty of healthy, fun friendships can grow out of other parts of our lives—such as mutual interests or shared activities. For instance, you're probably friends with some of the parents of your kids' classmates, or the people you regularly see at the gym. But the core relationships in our lives need to come from something deeper and more essential. If you really want to grow in Christ and accomplish God's purposes in your lives, then you need to invite God's presence into your relationships.

What are some practical ways to build a friendship on a solid faith foundation? The simplest answer is just to make every effort to be involved in each other's spiritual lives. Get to know your friends, ministry team members, or co-workers.

Here are just a few practical, everyday ways to foster the spiritual dimension of a relationship:

✟ Pray regularly for each other's' needs

✟ Study the Bible together

✟ Talk to each other about God's call on your lives

✟ Be honest about challenges weaknesses that you're struggling with

✟ Last, but certainly not least, make it a priority to have some fun together! Your relationship doesn't need to be all prayer meetings and Bible studies. Take some time to get to know each other's' hobbies and interests as well—it will add an extra dimension of familiarity to your relationship.

But the possibilities are endless—there are so many other ways, beyond the ones I've listed above, that you can use to develop a spiritual dimension to your relationships.

PRINCIPLE #2: *HUMILITY*

During our discussion of authenticity, Brad shared one of the most challenging and uncomfortable situations he's ever encountered as a Christian leader.

"Here I am sitting at the top of the Christian leadership landscape," he told me, remembering a time years ago when he and his team were doing some great things in the realm of Christian leadership training. "I remember my team, after winning some contests, buying me a gift in the form of dolls: one representing an angel, and one representing Satan.

The angel one was named 'Brad' and the Satan one was named 'Darb.' They confessed to me that they have been calling me 'Darb.' And this 'Darb' is the leader that we despise, who is so ambitious that he wants to run over others. That was a big lesson."

While Brad's experience definitely wasn't a pleasant one, it was a huge opportunity for spiritual growth. His team's words convicted him of a sin in his life he hadn't realised was there before, and motivated him to turn that part of his life around. Out of that difficult confrontation, Brad learned that being proud or overconfident in your own abilities can be one of the biggest hindrances to building an authentic relationship with others.

A great leader builds relationships through humility, and never thinks of him or herself as being more important than the people who support them. If the members of your team don't feel comfortable being honest with you about their concerns or asking questions about your leadership, then maybe it's time to spend some time thinking about humility.

PRINCIPLE #3: *ACCOUNTABILITY*

Brad's "Darb" story also points out another key aspect of Christian authenticity: a willingness to hold each other accountable for our actions. It probably wasn't easy for Brad's team to confront him about the issues they had with his over-ambition, but they did it anyway because they truly cared about him and valued his leadership. Conversely, it wasn't easy for Brad to accept their criticism, but he did so because he realised its value.

There are two sides to accountability: being brave enough to confront someone, and being humble enough to accept someone else's criticism of your behaviour. Both are equally important, because in a healthy Christian relationship both parties should feel free to speak honestly with each other. In fact, the Bible even tells us that we ought to "Therefore confess your sins to each other and pray for each other so that you may be healed." (James 5:16, NIV)

Imagine how hard it must have been for Brad's team to tell him about their concerns. Nonetheless, they took the time to deliver their message in a loving way and connected with him on a personal, private level rather than complaining about him behind his back. When you're confronting a friend about an issue you see in their life, avoid being confrontational or passive-aggressive. Present the issue at hand as plainly as you see it, but be sure to always speak out of gentleness and Christlike love.

After Brad's team confronted him, he did quite a lot of serious self-examination. "I asked myself: 'Am I going to be self-aware enough to take this and learn from it?'" he shared. "And 'Am I going to be vulnerable enough to allow this to blow up and be mad? Or am I going to be transparent, and thank them for pushing back on me and allowing me to see this blind-spot on my leadership journey?'"

At this point, Brad was asking all the right questions. He understood his team's concerns, and he took the time to prayerfully and critically think about how he was going to respond rather than reacting immediately out of hurt. This is a great example how to act when confronted with a loving, genuine criticism. Don't get angry or defensive, or lash out at your friends or co-workers: remember that they're most likely bringing this issue to your attention because they care about your Christian journey.

PRINCIPLE #4: *AVAILABILITY*

This is one of the more mundane aspects of Christian relationships, but it's still very important. If you want to build authenticity and trust in your relationships, you simply must be there for people when they need you. Sometimes this sort of consistent availability is difficult—after all, we all have busy schedules and a lot of responsibilities on our plates. But, if you really stop to think about it, how many things are more important than caring for the people God has placed in your life?

Let your friends know that you'll be there for them if they need your help, advice, or prayer. Knowing that each of you is a top priority in the others' life will radically deepen your relationship.

This quality has added importance for those of us in leadership positions, because everyone on your team expects you to be open and available to them as often as you can. Make a habit of having an "open-door" policy, and encourage your team to come to you with any questions or struggles they might have. Doing this will assure others that you're committed to their success as well as your own.

PRINCIPLE #5: *ENCOURAGEMENT*

In the book of Ephesians in the Bible, the apostle Paul encouraged church members to spend time building each other up in the Spirit. *"Do not let any unwholesome talk come out of your mouths,"* he writes, "*but only what is helpful for building others up according to their needs, that it may benefit those who listen." (Ephesians 4:29, NIV)*

It's hard to overestimate the power of a well-timed word of encouragement. If you take a few minutes to think about it, there's probably been a time that you can remember that a brother or sister in Christ reached out to you with a kind comment or helping hand. A good leader makes every effort to provide this sort of Godly encouragement, especially to the people they work with.

The first step to providing encouragement is to take a genuine interest in the lives of those around you. Notice that a co-worker has being looking a little tired recently? See that a member of your ministry team has been going through a difficult family situation recently? Then reach out to them. You simply cannot provide encouragement to someone if you don't know what is going on in their life—so the next time that you ask a friend how they're doing, really listen to their response. Then reach out with encouragement.

Everyone receives encouragement in different ways. Some people are buoyed by a gentle compliment or a friendly smile. Some people find great encouragement in thoughtful gifts or praise. And for some people, the best kind of encouragement is just quality time that lets them know that they are valued. As a leader, you know the personalities and values of the people around you. Use that knowledge to figure out how you can best offer encouragement in times of difficulty.

PRINCIPLE #6: *BRUTAL HONESTY*

Sometimes we all need some "real talk" in our lives, and an authentic Christian friend is often the very best person to give it! Brad shared with me some of the questions that he routinely asks his closest friends, both about his personal journey and his capacities as a leader. "In the authenticity area," he said, "I ask my inner circle: what I can get better at? What am I good at?" Brad always asks his friends to help him "celebrate one thing, and kick my butt on one thing."

It's great to have conversations like this with our friends from time to time, where we ask each other to honestly evaluate our behaviour. Don't be afraid to ask each other tough questions: this is your opportunity to receive critique from someone who values your spiritual wellbeing and your walk with Christ. Ask specific questions:

✝ Do you see me treating others with respect?

✝ Are there areas where I'm falling short of my full potential at work?

✝ Where do you think God is calling me to focus my gifts?

Be willing to answer their questions as well, and to do so as honestly as you can. Trust runs both ways. If you want someone to give you honest feedback about how you're doing, you should extend the same kind of genuine, gentle criticism to them as well.

Hopefully, some of Brad's insights have given you some practical ideas about how to cultivate authentic relationships. Think about these principles in relation to the friendships you have right now. How can you work today to make those friendships stronger?

As a recap, here are some of the steps to authentic relationships that we have covered in this chapter:

✝ Be practically involved in each other's spiritual development

✝ Don't allow pride to interfere with your relationship

✝ Hold each other accountable for your behaviour

✝ Be available for each other

✞ Provide understanding and encouragement

✞ Remain honest

Chapter 18

CELEBRATE OUR DIFFERENCES

We live on an incredibly diverse planet, rich in a variety of different lan-guages, cultures, and traditions. And each individual member of these thousands of cultures is a totally unique person, full of dreams and quirks and secret hopes for the future. No one is quite the same. All these differences are an integral part of God's plan for our world—after all, if everyone were the same, our lives would be quite boring!

Lee Jackson and Rev. Tim Roberts are two leaders who understand the unique power of diversity. Both men have served and spoken across the globe, and have a deep wealth of knowledge about the value of cultural and personal differences, in both the spiritual and business worlds.

Over the years, Lee has spoken in locations all over the world, where he loves sharing his strategies about how to be more productive at work and school. Nothing energises him more than being in front of a large audience. Today, Lee is a Fellow in the Professional Speaking Association, and the President of the organisation's Yorkshire chapter. He's also the author of six best-selling books, including *PowerPoint Surgery* and *The Business of Professional Speaking*, with which he hopes to share valuable insights about education and workplace efficiency.

Rev. Tim Roberts has served in churches in various parts of the world, including the southern United States, Honduras, Jamaica, Nicaragua, and Guatemala. He has visited 34 different countries during his ministry, and now serves alongside his wife Helen as the Senior Minister of Wellspring Church in Watford, where he uses his talents to provide visionary, strategic congregational leadership. Tim has a passion for learning about other cultures, healing inter-denominational conflicts, and understanding how best to minister to people from other cultures.

In my conversations with Lee and Tim, both men shared great insights about fostering diversity and dealing with interpersonal conflict. Their ideas greatly helped me in understanding these concepts, and I hope the same will be true for you.

DIFFERENCE #1: *CULTURE*

One of the factors that most greatly influences people's beliefs and behaviours is their culture. It's easy to underestimate the massive effect that our upbringing and socialisation have on the ways that we think about and interact with the world around us. This is especially true in our increasingly globalised world, where some of the lines between cultures have grown increasingly indistinct: today, many people consider themselves members of more than one culture, and it's quite possible for the average person to come into contact with 100's of different people each day.

As leaders, we should think of this situation as an awesome opportunity to influence others. Today, we can walk through a major city and hear dozens of different languages from all over the world. Right now, in fact, you can probably think of a few cultures other than your own that you have regular interactions with. We have an opportunity to spread ideas all over the world that no other generation has ever been blessed with. But our multicultural world also presents a very unique set of challenges, especially to leaders and influencers. In order to be effective in our positions in ministry or business in such a culturally diverse landscape, we must cultivate a sense of cultural awareness.

Tim Roberts certainly has experience in dealing with people from very different cultures. In fact, he identified this as one of the major challenges in his ministry. But through the years, Tim has learned how best to handle these challenges and to build trusting and fruitful relationships with people from other cultures.

The very first thing to do is rid your mind of any stereotypes or assumptions you may have formed about the culture in question. It is easy for these ideas to creep into our outlook, especially if you don't have personal relationships with people in this culture. Sometimes we aren't even aware of the preconceptions we may hold toward people of a certain culture or ethnicity. Unfortunately, the truth is that many of these stereotypes are based on fear, rather than love.

This attitude of fear is certainly not something we find in the Bible. In fact, the apostle Paul cautioned the early church about cultural divisions:

So in Christ Jesus you are all children of God through faith, for all of you who were baptised into Christ have clothed yourselves with Christ. There is neither Jew nor Gentile, neither slave nor free, nor is there male and female, for you are all one in Christ Jesus.

—GALATIANS 3:26-28

From this passage, we can see that God obviously views people of all cultures with equal respect. As His representatives in the marketplace and ministry, it is our responsibility to extend this Godly attitude toward people from other cultures.

If you don't have many friends from other cultures, then find some! Ask them questions about customs or beliefs that interest you, but always remember to be sensitive and respectful. Do your research in other ways, too: try reading books or blogs written from different cultural perspectives, or find other ways to respectfully engage with traditions that are not your own. In addition, understand that most people view their culture as an essential part of their identity. The same is probably true of you—we all have celebrations, traditions, and beliefs that we hold very dear to our hearts. Remember that, for those who have grown up in different cultural contexts, some of your traditions and beliefs may seem as strange as theirs seem to you.

Tim also points out that different cultural groups also need to be approached in different ways, particularly in ministry situations, in order to build healthy relationships. As leaders, we need to tailor our leadership styles to communicate effectively and politely with people whose customs may differ significantly from your own. "We all have a ministry to our Samaria," Tim said. (By "Samaria," he means unfamiliar cultures.) Rev. Roberts believes that engagement with other cultures is absolutely essential to the Christian leader's journey. "You cannot be a mature believer and follower of Christ and not care about the nations," he said. "It's possible for every believer to have some connection with the ends of the earth." So don't assume that full-time missions is the only way to engage meaningfully with other cultures—in today's global society, no one has an excuse not to get involved!

"Unity is an end in itself," Rev. Roberts shared. "What we're painted as a picture in the Scriptures is that, when mission has finished, what is left is united worship." All cultures will someday be united in this vast celebration. It is our job as Christian leaders to begin that unification here in the world.

What is Rev. Roberts' ideal vision for his organisation? "People of difference who are united. They don't lose their identity, they don't cease to be diverse: unity is difference united together. So we need to celebrate those differences," he said. "The Kingdom of Heaven is difference brought together."

DIFFERENCE #2: *PERSONALITY*

One of the most difficult challenges leaders will face is negotiating conflicts, many of which come from clashes between different kinds of personalities. "The biggest challenge for me is always people: dealing with people and trying to understand them," Lee offered when we spoke. "I've worked with people in the past who were not really like me, and understanding their personality was a challenge. Life's all about relationships," he added. But he also said that it can be hard to figure out people's behaviour: "You're trying to get behind why they're saying that, why they're doing that."

From a leadership perspective, it is often helpful to understand the different personality types you may have in your team. Psychologically-focused personality profiles—such as the Myers-Briggs Personality Test—can offer extremely valuable insights into the way that people think about the world. Though such tests certainly aren't perfect, they can still shed light on how dramatically our perspectives differ from others'. For instance, some people perceive events in a very logical, factual way, while others focus more on their instincts and feelings. Some people are more introverted, and frequently need time on their own to relax; others are more extroverted, and get their energy from spending time with others. Having a more complete picture of your team members' personalities will help you understand how to help them become happier and more productive.

Of course, we will still meet people whose personalities seem unpredictable, people who keep surprising us even after we have known them for a very long time. Sometimes this is a wonderful surprise—but sometimes it isn't. For Lee, this is where the concept of Biblical grace comes into play. He tries his best to extend understanding and mercy when others seem cranky or ill-tempered. "Sometimes people have bad days," he said. "And you just need to let them have a bad day, say 'I'm going to back off now.'" The ability to step back and not take things too personally is a mark of great maturity. Leaders often manage people who are going through stressful or high-pressure situations, so this skill can prove invaluable.

What is Lee's best advice for "getting along" with the people on your team? "Relate to them with understanding," Lee said. "Be real, authentic, and have integrity." A great leader treats others with kindness and respect, even those whose personalities differ greatly from their own.

As an example, Lee shared with me a story of working alongside another speaker who was behaving strangely before an event. Through asking some gentle questions, Lee was able to figure out that the other speaker was finding it difficult to concentrate due to some agitation they had about the upcoming event. "I could have reacted to that badly, and it could have gone a different way. But I chose not to do that." In the end, Lee was able to pray with the other speaker and help them get through a difficult day. Imagine if Lee had responded with harshness or judgment instead of understanding! But because he took the time to show grace toward another person's suffering, Lee was able to show Godly kindness during another person's suffering.

DIFFERENCE #3: *SPIRITUAL GIFTS*

Another key difference between people is the spiritual gifts that each of us has received. God has given everyone a unique set of capabilities and sensitivities, which He uses to enable us to do important work in the world. In one of his letters, the apostle Paul encouraged the early church members to embrace people who had many different spiritual talents:

> *To one there is given through the Spirit a message of wisdom, to another a message of knowledge by means of the same Spirit, to another faith by the same Spirit, to another gifts of healing by that one Spirit, to another miraculous powers, to another prophecy, to another distinguishing between spirits, to another speaking in different kinds of tongues, and to still another the interpretation of tongues. All these are the work of one and the same Spirit, and he distributes them to each one, just as he determines. Just as a body, though one, has many parts, but all its many parts form one body, so it is with Christ.*

—I Corinthians 15:8-12

There is a sometimes a difficult lesson to be learned here, about the diversity that God wants us to cultivate in our churches and businesses. Imagine if you had five noses but no hands—life would be a lot more difficult, wouldn't it? That is exactly what an organisation looks like when people who have certain spiritual gifts are excluded, or preference is given to others. An ideal leader will welcome people with many different talents—in that way, team members can cover for each other's' weaknesses and be encouraged by each other's' strengths.

177

Diversity is God's ideal situation, in any area of life. Businesses and ministries that are intentionally welcoming to people from many different cultures will become healthier and more dynamic as a result. So as leaders, it is our responsibility to celebrate differences in the teams we lead.

To wrap up, here are some of the concepts we've spoken about in this chapter:

✝ Educate yourself about other cultures

✝ Don't make assumptions based on a person's culture or ethnicity

✝ Engage with your "Samaria"

✝ Understand the personality types you have on your team

✝ Treat others with respect and understanding

✝ Value other people's spiritual gifts, and understand that God gives everyone different skills and talents

✝ Above all: celebrate unity through diversity!

One of your most important jobs as a leader is to help people over-come the persistent, discouraging myths that they hear from society every day. We have a powerful, God-ordained influence over the people we lead, and it is our responsibility to speak Biblical truths into their lives. If we as Christian leaders do not do this important work, then who will?

Dr. John Muratori is a Christian leader who speaks powerfully on the topic of combatting society's lies. Dr. Muratori has had an impressive career as a speaker, author, and management and financial consul-tant. His Biblically-centered economics curriculum, *Money By Design,* is a staple at churches, schools, and businesses across the world, and continues to revolutionise the Christian perspective on money. His consulting firm, City Ink, has helped clients from large corporations to small churches rethink their management and marketing strategies.

Through the years, Dr. Muratori has worked with clients as diverse as the United States Department of Homeland Security and the Department of Mental Health. He also serves as the Executive Director of the Turning Point Christian Centre, a substance abuse treatment centre, whose innovative and highly successful methods have set the national standard for Christian rehabilitation programs.

In recent years, Dr. Muratori has also found his calling as the Senior Pastor of Calvary Life Family Worship Centre, a multi-campus nonde-nominational church with sites in Connecticut and Texas. Today, he travels the world speaking on topics such as leadership and social media marketing, and is well-known as a thoughtful, energising, and innovative thinker.

As you might expect from someone with so much experience and ini-tiative, Dr. Muratori's thoughts on Christian leadership and influence showed a lot of wisdom. From his years of experience in the marketplace and the church, he has gleaned a number of insights about how to dispel society's most common myths.

In this chapter, I'd like to talk about some of the most common lies that we hear from modern society. We'll speak about how to combat these myths in our own lives, and how to lead by example in our businesses and ministries.

MYTH #1: "YOU WEREN'T MEANT FOR GREATNESS!"

Of all the lies that we regularly hear from our society, this is one of the most pervasive and tragic. It robs Christians of our vision, our passion, and our effectiveness in the world. To make matters worse, everyone is susceptible, even those who seem the most confident in their faith.

Many influences, from the advertisements we see in magazines to the business associates we work with every day to the popular movies and television shows we watch, constantly bombard us with images of mediocrity. "Just settle down," we hear every day. "There's nothing more to life than going to work and having some fun on the weekends. You'll never make a *real* difference in the world," these voices say. In this world, doing great things is reserved for the people who have money, popularity, and influence. Think about it this way: it is in many people's interest for the majority of us to be content with mediocrity. Society tells us that it might be possible for a few people to bring about real change in the world, but to believe that you're one of them is just absurd—right?

As Dr. Muratori shared with me: "Culturally, we're not trained to do great things. The society is mainly designed to keep people in their economic place, and society functions better—according to the elites—when people don't want to do great things." In short, it's in all these people's interest to make us think that "business as usual" is the only way things will ever be. Over time, this attitude creeps into the way that we think about ourselves as well: we start to believe that our lives will never amount to anything more than what we see around us every day.

But this kind of life is not what God wants for any of us! God created each person with a distinct and incredibly important purpose in life. Though we may not ever know His complete plan, to think that we'll just never amount to anything great is to doubt His work in our lives. Of course, this "greatness" looks different for everyone—God doesn't write one-size-fits-all plans! He will call some of us to positions of high power and influence and some of us to less glamorous work behind the scenes. But all of this work serves a valuable purpose in His plan. Not everyone is called to be a megachurch pastor or a flashy corporate executive. "We need to train people not to be pastors, and not to function in the church, but in society," Dr. Muratori said.

What are some of the ways that we can battle these destructive thoughts in our own lives? One of the best strategies is, of course, turning to the

Bible. In the book of John, when Jesus was telling His disciples about His plans on the earth, he gave them these powerful words:

> *You did not choose me, but I chose you and appointed you so that you might go and bear fruit—fruit that will last—and so that whatever you ask in my name the Father will give you. This is my command: Love each other.*

—John 15:16-17

What a completely different message from the one we hear every day! In this passage, we see that the Christian is called to a task far beyond any prosperity the world could possibly offer us, because this greatness will have eternal rewards. And this kind of life-changing, radical purpose certainly isn't reserved for the rich, famous, and conventionally "successful"—it's available to everyone who has faith in God's plans. He has already chosen us. It is up to you to return the favour. But Jesus wasn't finished quite yet. This passage continues to share some very valuable wisdom about the Christian's purpose in the world:

> *If the world hates you, keep in mind that it hated me first. If you belonged to the world, it would love you as its own. As it is, you do not belong to the world, but I have chosen you out of the world. That is why the world hates you.*

—John 15:18-19

Here, Christ is warning us that the Christian perspective is at odds with everything that our society will try to tell us. His words are especially true today, when so much of the world has grown hostile to the church and its teachings. We simply must make an effort not to unwittingly embrace society's ideology. God has blessed you with passions and talents for a reason. Through his power, you have the ability to genuinely impact the people around you.

So, are you consumed with a desire for authentic worship? Skilled in financial planning? Passionate about ministering to young parents? Have a daring idea for a new startup business? You can develop those skills and ideas into great successes. Don't let anyone discourage or dissuade you! If your calling comes from God, He will enable you to carry out His purposes in the world around you. This may not be society's picture of "greatness," but a calling much higher, whose influence will reach into eternity. Why settle for mediocrity in this world when you could have greatness in God's eyes?

Getting rid of this attitude in your own life is one thing, but it's often more difficult to help others overcome this kind of negative thinking. It can be incredibly difficult to get an accurate picture of your own potential. So how can a Christian leader help others to see what they're capable of?

"Get people to see God's DNA in their life—to be trailblazers, to be unique, to be the kind of person God wants them to be!" Dr. Muratori encouraged. "It's important to us to give the gospel with no bondage." By this, he means that Christian leaders should focus on empowering people to discover their own potential. We shouldn't load them down with expectations about what we think they should be pursuing, or try to tell them what God has planned for their lives. Rather, we should encourage them to discover their own gifts and purpose.

Remember that not everyone has the same sort of gifts and skills. One person might be called to full-time ministry, while another might find fulfilment in a high-powered business career. For this reason, Dr. Muratori places a high value on "trying to get people to see their leadership dynamic in their spheres." As Christian leaders, it is our privilege (and our responsibility) to show people that they can change the world.

MYTH #2: *"THERE'S ALWAYS A LITTLE MORE!"*

The flip side of the "Mediocrity Myth" is another one of society's favourite lies: that everybody wants to "have it all." The world loves to tell us that since we will never achieve great things, we will need to be content with simply owning a lot of "stuff." Instead of finding fulfilment in living wisely or following God's call, this cultural narrative tells us that we should find that satisfaction in material goods and experiences.

Marketing agencies that try to sell us expensive televisions and designer clothes want us to believe that we can't be fulfilled without having a lot of "stuff." Companies that want us to buy their products want to tell us that we won't be happy without the newest, shiniest goods. But doing God's will often requires incredible material sacrifices. Think of some of the greatest leaders in the Bible, people like Daniel, Joseph of Egypt, and Jesus' disciples. All of these people sacrificed their material possessions—and often their entire lifestyle—just to do what God had asked them to do. If you think you might be struggling with this cultural myth, consider reflecting on the following questions.

What are the most important "things" in my life? Are they material, or spiritual?

✝ Where do I spend the majority of my dispensable income?

✝ Would I give up my lifestyle to obey God's plans for me?

✝ Are there any possessions that I feel like I couldn't get rid of? Why?

✝ What do I spend most of my free time pursuing?

Perhaps the answers to these questions will point out some of the places where you're prioritising your lifestyle above your spiritual maturity. Thoughtfully considering where you invest your time, money, and passion is the first step to rearranging your priorities. Many of us who are driven leaders and innovators enjoy a great deal of material success. But these blessings should never become more important than our relationship with Christ. Set an example for the people under your leadership through your humility.

In his letter to the church leader Timothy, Paul gave this valuable advice about Christians and money:

> *Command those who are rich in this present world not to be arrogant nor to put their hope in wealth, which is so uncertain, but to put their hope in God, who richly provides us with everything for our enjoyment. Command them to do good, to be rich in good deeds, and to be generous and willing to share. In this way they will lay up treasure for themselves as a firm foundation for the coming age, so that they may take hold of the life that is truly life.*

—I Timothy 6:17-19

As Jesus often told us, there is no need to worry about possessions. What's more important is our sense of purpose and our commitment to Godly living. Trust in God's provision, not in society's lies.

MYTH #3: *"STICK TO WHAT YOU KNOW!"*

Dr. Muratori has obviously been successful in many different areas of life, but what advice does he give to everyone? According to Dr. Muratori, the daily practice of mental engagement has been a revolutionary force in his life. In fact, he shared some very simple habits that have helped to take him beyond the ordinary. One thing he strongly emphasises is becoming committed to personal growth.

"I'm an avid learner. I love to learn, I love to read," he said about his daily routine. "I think a portion of my success is due to the fact that I'm always learning. I'm always looking to learn," he told me. "And I think the Lord has allowed me to see His principles in various fields." From early in his career, Dr. Muratori has made a habit of cracking open a book at least once daily, usually something written on a subject about which he isn't already well-informed. He finds that this helps him develop new skills and remain fascinated by God's incredible creation.

Sadly, we live in a world that discourages us from branching out and educating ourselves to our full potential. We're told that once our education at school is finished, we should find an occupation in our field and stick to it. Because of this cultural attitude most people sadly don't prioritise learning, or stick to the few topics they already enjoy, rather than learning about new subjects.

Dr. Muratori definitely doesn't follow this cultural pattern. In fact, he believes that intellectual curiosity is one of the hallmarks of a great Christian leader. "Go outside what you're currently doing to read," he advised everyone who wants to refine their leadership capacities. "Educate yourself in different fields, whether it's psychology, astronomy, woodworking, automotive science, or whatever else." Think of the potential benefits: perhaps you'll discover a new hobby, develop an interest in a new field of study, gain knowledge you can pass on to others, or even plant the seeds for a new ministry or career in your future. Even better, you'll be setting a great example for those under your leadership. Nothing will encourage and edify your team more than watching you make a consistent effort to better yourself.

In addition, Dr. Muratori recommends using Bible memorisation as a tool to keep your mind lively and sharp. Committing verses to your mind not only helps engage your brain, but also actively contributes to the strength of your spiritual life. Memorise a few passages, and you'll be surprised at how quickly they come to mind when you're struggling with a spiritual issue or just having a difficult day. There is no better antidote to society's lies than the healing truth of God's word.

One of the most crucial keys to lifelong learning is consistency. Dr. Muratori makes sure to take time every day devoting himself to serious, intentional study. "When we learn something, it ignites a spark," Dr. Muratori shared. "The difference between a genius and an average person is that a genius is always, always learning." So if you want to revitalise your attitude about life and add a few new skills to your leadership toolkit, take some time out of every single day to focus on further developing your knowledge. It's never too late to hit the books!

To review, here are some of the tools we've reviewed for dispelling society's most common myths:

✝ Trust that God has created you for greatness

✝ Don't be discouraged from your calling and passion

✝ Encourage others to see "God's DNA" in their lives

✝ Seek fulfilment in spiritual growth, not material possessions

✝ Read, read, read—never stop learning

✝ Measure everything you hear from society against God's truth

The ability to get the best out of the people you lead

| FOCUS ON THE ESSENTIALS

In the book of Proverbs, Chapter 29:18, the Bible tells us: "Where there is no vision, the people perish." For many churches, as well as business organisations, this verse holds a key to real growth that many leaders in the church and marketplace often miss.

When it comes to administration, productivity, and team growth, vision is one hundred percent essential. There is no way around it. If you do not have a clear **vision** as a leader, you and your team will never grow. Without vision, leaders will find their days to be less productive, essentially walking along a path with no destination in mind, making it impossible to reach any destination at all. In this chapter, I am excited to share some thoughts with you on vision that I learned from a great man and church leader, Bil Cornelius.

Bil is the lead pastor and founder of a church in Corpus Christi, Texas, called Church Unlimited. Bil's church hosts 10 campuses and around 9,000 members spread across different locations throughout Texas. After seventeen years now in ministry, Bil's priceless knowledge of lead-ership principles have propelled him and his church to great success. Of all the lessons he has learned however, Bil believes that having a clear vision is crucial as you start out on your journey of leadership - and that is exactly where he started all those years ago.

As a young adult, Bil attended a non-Christian state college, where he met many "unchurched" students on campus. As he talked with them and got to hear more of their thoughts about Jesus and the church, he found his unique calling as a future pastor. After graduation, Bil moved to Corpus Christi with his wife and newly-born son to start the church God had helped him to envision. As a young couple with few funds at their disposal, Bil and his wife started their church with five people in their small apartment.

While he didn't know where the funds were going to come from, or how God would grow the church he had envisioned, Bil felt strongly that he was called to lead "unchurched" people into fellowship with Christ. So he set out to seek God for more answers. What he found was the need for a greater vision.

Remember that the keys to creating and leading with a clear vision that I'm about to share with you can apply to any leader, in any position. So, with that in mind, let's take a closer look at these four key ideas that Bil shared with me about how as a Christian Leader he leads with a clear vision.

THE FIRST KEY: 100 HOURS OF PRAYER

As a Christian leader, whether in the church or business world, it is always important that we hear from God and seek His will first. "The vision should come from God," Bil told me, not from the pastor or anyone else. But where does this true vision come from, and how do we seek it out from God?

We must seek him in our prayer time.

When Bil was first starting out, in his fairly small church, he had a life-changing conversation with God. While on a weekend trip with his wife, Bil visited a series of theme parks, where he watched a short film on the life of Walt Disney. At the end of this film, Bil was inspired by a thought from God. God told him: "If a man can do this with a mouse, what can you do with the Holy Spirit?"

After hearing this from God, Bil felt led to pray and ask God how many hours he should commit to praying about the vision for his church. At first he was willing to pray for 20 hours, then asked God if that was enough. God told him to keep praying about it, so he did. This continued over the next few days, during which Bil prayed over eight hours for an answer. Finally, Bil heard a clear answer from God: in fact, God physically showed him a statue in one of the parks he visited that had a giant number on top of it. The number was 100.

"How about praying 100 hours?" God asked Bil. (Apparently, the park was celebrating the one hundredth anniversary of Disney World at the time.) While 100 hours seemed too much at first, Bil agreed to pray for a vision and made the commitment that God had asked of him.

That decision alone changed the course of Bil's ministry and propelled his church into huge growth over the next few years. When he first started praying, Bil heard nothing from God. He reached the Ten-hour mark, then twenty and thirty, then forty. Still nothing. But Bill persisted in keeping his promise, and finally, around the fifty-hour mark, he started to hear and see a vision. In his spirit, he saw people from all over the world, each from a different culture, walking up to him to ask him a single question: "When are you going to start the church that will change *my* life?" He saw people from Africa, Europe, South America, and many other parts of the world, all asking him this exact question. That was when Bil knew that his church was called to fund and plant new churches all around the world. That was the clear vision that he received from God.

To this day, Bil's church is fulfilling that vision by supporting many church plants both in the United States and around the world. This story is just one of many from which leaders everywhere can glean wisdom about the importance of prayer.

As leaders, none of us will ever outgrow the need for prayer. However, after we pray and receive vision for our businesses and ministries, we must **take action** to move forward and bring these visions to pass. We must learn and apply productive leadership activities that guide these visions from far-away pictures in our minds and spirits into the realm of reality.

According to Bil, two main keys that he's learned over the years have helped bring his church massive growth and allowed him to achieve greater productivity. These two keys are: *Friend-Raising* (or Fund Raising) and something he calls the *Quality of Worship* rule.

THE SECOND KEY: *FRIEND-RAISING*

As any pastor or business leader understands, bringing your vision into reality requires having funds. You need money and resources to start a business, plant a new church, and support missions and outreaches. Once you receive a vision for your organisation, your next step is to find the funds to bring that vision to pass. Bil has learned how to acquire these funds through a process he calls *"friend-raising."*

In Bil's concept, "friend-raising" is simply building relationships with people who could potentially fund a certain project and help make your vision a reality. Bil told me that he takes time each and every day to build relationships with people who can also be thought of as *key donors*. He does this by going out to lunch with these people or talking with them over the phone. One thing that Bil does *not* do, however, is ask anyone for money directly. He does not target people and build fake relationships with them just to raise funds for his church projects.

Instead, Bil simply shares his vision and what is on his heart, at the moment, when it comes to his ministry and the Lord's will for his projects. As Christian leaders, God works to bring people into our lives that can help fund the vision for the ministries we lead. In fact, the Bible says:

> *For where your treasure is, there your heart will be also.*

> —LUKE 12:24 (NIV)

In light of this verse, Bil believes strongly that if you share your heart openly with key donors and allow God to work in their hearts as well, God will always lead the right people to sow into your ministry. Great leaders make time to build relationships with these people. If you practice Bil's "friend-raising" strategy, you will soon find that there is more than enough provision for your vision.

THE THIRD KEY: GROWTH IN NUMBERS

Now that we have covered how to receive a vision from God, and ways to fund your vision, let me share with you another revelation about growth that Bil told me he has learned. Although Bil is always concerned with how many people he is reaching for Christ and who are entering heaven more than he is about his overall church attendance, he believes that numbers are still important. In fact, over the years Bil has come to learn a few administrative secrets that can either hinder or encourage growth.

In a young church (or business), Bil always tells leaders about something he calls "*The 0-200 Rule.*"

Here's the concept behind this rule. When a church's attendance ranges from 0 to 200 people in total, those people are attending the church for only one reason: to socialise. In other words, people are showing up each week because they like seeing each other—even more than they like the sermons or enjoy the live band. Although that may seem like a negative statement, Bil has found this principle to be true of many churches. If you stop and think about it, churches that have only 200 members or less usually have less funding and resources than other, more established churches. In light of this, elements like the quality of the church's praise-and-worship band and the effectiveness of its administration are often lacking in overall quality. This idea brings us to the next level of growth leaders must conquer: *the quality of worship*, or the quality of the atmosphere.

THE FOURTH KEY: QUALITY OF WORSHIP AND ATMOSPHERE

Once a church or business grows beyond 200 members, Bil believes that its dynamics shift. In the church, Bil calls this shift "the worship barrier." Every church goes through this initial worship barrier once it passes the 200-member mark. After you have more than two hundred members it is not possible for the pastor, or any staff member, to connect on a personal level with every member.

For example, if you look at your contacts list on your phone, you will see that list probably contains about 200 people that you know at a personal level. These are people like friends and family members, and possibly work colleagues. Beyond that, the rest of our contacts are just acquaintances. The same is true in a larger church body. At this point in a church, Bil explained, the leadership has to offer more to people than just the bare minimum.

Why? Because when you surpass 200 members, people will start coming and staying for a different reason altogether: the quality of worship. This term generally refers to the whole atmosphere, or the way the church presents itself to the people who attend. In a church setting, the atmosphere may include elements like the excellence of the singers and musicians in the band, the engagement level of the sermons, and the quality of community outreaches and children's programs.

Obviously, this concept can and should apply in the marketplace as well. In a business, the quality level shown to clients and staff will say a lot about the leadership and potential for growth. As an example, let's say you were a potential client meeting staff of an organisation in their office for the first time. If the staff members were inappropriately dressed, the office space was disorganised, and it seemed that no one was prepared for the meeting, you would probably not wish to do business with that company.

So the same rule applies inside and outside the church: everything must be done with quality and excellence. This is why when you reach 300+ members, Bil says that you have to do things differently.

Administratively, this can be a hard process for both pastoral staff and other church leaders. This is a process that may require the pastor to let some members of staff go and to hire others who fit the current needs of the body. Take a musician as an example. Bil told me that because his vision is to be a church for the unchurched, he leads so as to seriously compete with other opportunities in the world, such as the clubs and bars down the street. In essence, he believes that if we want to keep people coming into the church, we have to offer them something of real quality— so if a musician or singer on the worship team doesn't look good, sound good, and add something to the team, then the pastoral leadership may have to make a hard decision and find someone else who can do the job better. Your team and staff simply must be the best of the best if you want to move forward with a vision that is greater than one person. And every vision from God is bigger than one individual. That's why, unfortunately, not everyone who starts at your side will stay with your vision to the end.

As Bil told me: "It is okay not to be liked, but it is not okay to miss God's plan." It is always more important to hear from God and lead with his vision than to lead a crowd blindly into nothing. Get clear on your vision— then run with it!

To recap, here are the keys we have covered in this chapter:

✝ Pray consistently for a vision

✝ Lead with that clear vision in mind

✝ Build strong relationships with donors ("friend-raise")

✝ Apply "quality of worship" principles with your staff and leadership teams

✝ Focus on God's plan and believe for growth

Chapter 21

CREATE A CULTURE THAT PRODUCES RESULTS

Even leaders and administrators who have a clear vision of where they're going often find that getting there is harder than they anticipated. In fact, many of the challenges we face along the way are not only unexpected, but simply cannot be avoided. The main problem that many of us face is finding a way to keep producing quality results while we're figuring out solutions to these challenges. In short, how do we deal with unexpected challenges without minimising our team's productivity?

One solution, which I learned from business genius Perry Marshall, is to take control of your business's culture. Great leaders get the results they want because they are the architects of culture in their ministries, businesses, and lives. So, how do we take control of the culture and the environment?

Beginning this process is as simple as removing any barriers that would stunt overall team growth. In the same way that an architect designs and envisions a building before it comes into existence, it is our job as leaders to have a clear vision of our organisation's end goal. If you've followed some of the keys from the first chapter, then you already have a good idea of some of the best ways to accomplish this step of the process.

Many of the barriers that we must overcome in order to grow are mental. Again, it helps to think about this concept in terms of construction. Before an architect can do his job properly, builders and engineers must come along and clear the land, survey the property, and organise paperwork before construction can even begin. As leaders, clearing out a space to work is just as important as drafting the blueprints—and it is our job to do both.

In business and life, many of us are holding ourselves back by believing lies that have been fed to us by our modern culture. These lies then grow into our mental philosophies and the truths we believe about ourselves, our businesses, and the marketplace. You would be surprised at how often these internal beliefs can either make or break your personal life and work.

In light of this, understanding your *kingdom identity*, and how it relates to the culture in your work and life, is one of the most powerful truths you will ever learn about successful leadership. Without understanding your identity as a leader, you will be unable to take charge of the culture in your life and business.

According to Perry Marshall, "mixing kingdom and marketplace business can be tricky" for Christian leaders. And he's right.

Fortunately, however, we do not have to make the same mistakes that other leaders before us have made. So let's take a look at one of the most pervasive lies about Christian leadership and find out how to debunk this lie, and others.

THE LIE OF "SECOND-CLASS"

One of the biggest lies being taught inside and outside of the church is that if you are a businessman or woman you are somehow "second-class" to the rest of the body of believers.

Perry Marshall is a devout Christian and a highly sought-after Internet marketing entrepreneur. He is one of the most expensive consultants in the fields of sales, engineering, and psychology, and has authored several best-selling books, such as *80/20 Sales and Marketing: The Definitive Guide to Working Less and Making More,* and the *Ultimate Guide to Google AdWords.*

The son of parents who worked in full time ministry, Perry struggled with feelings of inadequacy. Early in life, he knew that he was not called to pastoral ministry like his parents. Although he believed in God and began a personal relationship with him when he was a young child, Perry wanted to become a businessman. He was naturally curious, and excelled in math, science, and other subjects that eventually led him to work in engineering and marketing as a young adult.

Unfortunately, although Perry became very successful in his chosen career, he had to confront the same myth that misleads far too many of people both inside and outside of the church. Perry soon realised that this idea that believers who work outside traditional ministries are somehow second-class is simply ridiculous. Nonetheless this myth is devastating, particularly to young leaders.

Yet this lie has still kept many talented men and women outside the marketplace, away from their calling as business leaders. The simple truth is that traditional ministry is not for everyone. In fact, the Bible says:

> *And He Himself gave some to be apostles, some prophets, some evangelists, and some pastors and teachers.*

—Ephesians 4:11 (NKJV)

Clearly, not everyone in the church is meant to take on the same role.

As Perry sees it, the problem is that many people believe that this passage only applies directly to the church rather than to both the ministry and the marketplace. Perry, however, thinks otherwise: he believes that these forms of ministry exist just as much in the marketplace as they do inside the church.

If you actually look to the Gospels, you will see that great men and women of God were leaders in business before the modern church existed. Take the best-known Biblical figures as examples: Paul was a tent-maker; Daniel was a government administrator; Peter was a fisherman; and Joseph became second in command over all of Egypt! These men were great faith leaders, but they were also regular faces in the secular marketplace.

Based on this evidence, we can clearly see that leadership goes far beyond the church walls. If this is true, we must learn how to cultivate a productive mindset in our businesses and our personal lives that will in turn manifest the type of culture needed to fulfil our vision. Furthermore, as Christian leaders, we must aim to create God-honouring culture and environments within our businesses. This can only be done if we first tear down these lies that plague our mental road maps and steer us off course.

LEAVING THE IVORY TOWER

An ivory tower is in many senses much like a sacred cow that must be knocked over before one can move forward in a new mindset. As Perry shared, many believers in the modern Western church have sadly grown up in an ivory tower that is not connected with the real world around them. Unfortunately, this means that many believers' faith wavers after they reach adulthood and face the real challenges and obstacles of living in the world's culture. Perry's brother, who nearly lost his faith as a young adult, is a good example of this sad truth. Even though Perry's brother had graduated from seminary and lived in China as an undercover missionary, he almost ended his four years in the mission field as an atheist.

On the other hand, Perry—who has been working in the secular mar-ketplace for decades now—still has a strong belief in God and is a committed Christian. Why did the two men's experiences differ so greatly? How did a leader in the church come so close to losing his faith, while a leader in the marketplace held onto his so strongly?

If we are being honest, this is a tricky question to answer. I doubt that anyone of us has all the definite answers on this topic. However, there are some leadership strategies that you can use to create a Godly culture, either inside or outside the church. Perry shared some of these key culture-building strategies with me himself, and now I will share them with you.

STRATEGY #1: WALKING IN GODLY CHARACTER

Displaying character and integrity is something that people expect of their leaders, no matter the job or the situation. Leadership positions, whether in the full-time ministry or marketplace, are held to higher standards than other jobs. Furthermore, teams will reflect their leader's character in their principles and work ethic. As an example of this, Perry mentioned the story of a highly-paid politician from the United States who was accused of having an affair with a woman, and whose career was greatly damaged as a result.

Many of us assume that the values of the ministry and the marketplace are opposite to each other. But this is simply not true. Many people would have never tolerated this politician's dishonest behaviour if it had come from a CEO, as Perry pointed out. At the end of the day, if you want to be a successful leader in any industry, you must live your life in an upright manner. You must place a high value on honesty, truthfulness, and sincerity if you expect your success to last.

While this is true for any leader, the Bible features many examples of government leaders who were also men and women of God. By leading with Godly character and values, they stood out, were promoted in their positions of leadership, and were anointed by God.

Two of the best-known examples of these values are Daniel and Joseph. Joseph was thrown into prison for crimes he did not commit, and he was abandoned by his own family. In the midst of his struggles, however, Joseph still chose to do the right thing; he continued to behave with integrity and display a Godly character. In the end, he was promoted to second-in-command over all of Egypt. Pharaoh told him, *"You shall be over my house, and all my people shall order themselves as you command. Only as regards the throne will I be greater than you."* (Gen. 41:40 ESV)

Daniel, also a government administrator, received a promotion only after he was nearly executed for disobeying the king's orders and refusing to worship other gods. These two men are only two of the many examples of Godly leadership in the Bible, but the principles they demonstrated are still relevant in today's culture. If you are determined to become and remain a successful leader, leading by Godly example will prove to be a crucial part of reaching your goal.

STRATEGY #2: *CULTURAL VISION*

According to Perry, a business is a self-contained culture: each workplace has a different environment that trickles down from the leadership at the top. What does this mean for us as leaders? If we are not happy with the current environment in our companies and organisations, we ought to look in the mirror first. It is our job to align our workplace's culture with our vision. The best way to manage this is to make sure that we're clearly communicating that vision to our team members. Doing this ensures that our organisations will operate with more efficiency and more productivity, and that we will keep accomplishing tasks in pursuit of our vision.

As Christian leaders, we need to lead by example, create a culture within our businesses that reflect Godly principles, and encourage pursuit of the kingdom in the workplace.

At the core of this concept is an emphasis on bringing the Christian values to the marketplace. Lance Wallnau is the author of the book *Invading Babylon: The 7 Mountain Mandate*, which Perry highly recommends to leaders. In his book, Wallnau makes the case that modern Christians have tried so hard to keep the secular culture outside its walls that we have forgotten to take our church's culture out to the world.

If you look at most successful leaders, you will consistently see that their lifestyles reflect kingdom principles. They try to live honestly, they work diligently to take care of their families, and they lead their businesses with excellence. So, if you want to create a kingdom culture within your organisation, first assess your vision and see if its culture is in alignment with that vision.

STRATEGY #3: *THE SECRET TO SELLING*

Although it is clear that businesses are about more than just sales and numbers, it is obvious that selling is still a huge element—and ultimately the end goal—of any thriving business. So what is the secret to making sales? Perry shared with me a key ingredient to answering this question, a principle which surprisingly originates in the Bible.

At one time or another, Perry explained, we've all felt a little bit abandoned. Many of us are like orphans. This is why leading characters in many popular films, such as *Star Wars* and most Disney movies, are both motherless and fatherless. (Think of characters like Luke Skywalker and Snow White.) Whether we can no longer relate to friends, family or coworkers who don't share our dreams or enthusiasm, or have just never had assurance from a mentor, we've all felt abandoned at one time or another.

In the business world, people are the same. Most potential customers, clients, and buyers you are selling to are all looking to scratch that "orphan itch," to feel a little less abandoned. The goal in sales, then, should be to connect with our customers in a way that makes them no longer feel lonely or lost. As the Bible says in Galatians 4:5:

> *To redeem those who were under the law,*
> *that we might receive the adoption as sons.*

In the same way that Christ bridged the gap and facilitated our adoption as sons and daughters in his kingdom, great leaders must bridge the personal gaps between themselves, their staff, and their customers. Leading in accordance with Christlike principles will always produce the growth you're looking for. This can be done in many ways: just think of how much your business could grow if you focused more on making customers feel genuinely appreciated and valued. At the end of the day, making an authentic connection with clients is likely the best-kept sales secret.

When it comes to making sales, just remember that everyone has felt lost and abandoned. If we learn how to effectively fill those voids for our customers and staff, sales will become the easiest part of growing our businesses.

So far, we have discussed how important it is for us to leave our ivory towers, and adopt new mindsets for success. We have gone over three important strategies for gaining lasting success in the marketplace, and discussed why it is crucial to bring kingdom culture outside of the church walls and into the marketplace.

Lastly, after speaking with Perry about his ups and downs in the marketplace so far, I've come to realise that having wrong beliefs can destroy a business as easily as they can hurt us in life. The bottom line, then, is this: if we want to grow our businesses and our teams, we must first cultivate the right beliefs in our own mindset, and then guide our organisation's culture using those beliefs.

To recap, here are the keys we have covered in this chapter:

✙ Deconstructing harmful cultural lies is crucial to success

✙ Good leaders are also architects of their organisation's culture

✝ Kingdom business exists inside and outside of the church walls

✝ Belief is a powerful thing, and we must believe in our businesses and our callings

✝ Businessmen and women need to walk in Godly leadership to sustain lasting success

✝ We are *all* called to serve—and we are all first-class citizens of Heaven

Chapter 22

KEEP THE RIGHT PERSPECTIVE

Every leader agrees on one thing: leadership is hard. Whether you are a leader in a church, business, or both, answering the call of God and learning to lead can be a challenge for the best of us. Making a differ-ence while leading a ministry or business is always the end goal, but this task can feel impossible when you're trying to manage the fine details of your organisation while also keeping the "big picture" in mind. So how do we lead well and also keep Christ's purpose at the centre of our daily operations?

The answer is to walk in *humility*.

Humility can have many wonderful benefits for leaders: it keeps us grounded in our leadership roles, deepens our connection to God's plan, and continually renews our sense of purpose. For Les Isaac, this journey toward humility was crucial in his development as a believer and as a leader. After interviewing this powerful man of God, I found myself convinced that learning to serve humbly in every situation is not only the key to leadership success, but is also crucial to our Christian maturity. Humility is essential to fulfilling our missions with purpose.

Les Isaac is the CEO of the Christian charity Ascension Trust and the co-founder of an innovative project called the Street Pastors Initiative, which provides late- night outreaches to tackle the issue of guns, knives and violent crimes in high-crime areas in Britain, Australia, USA, Jamaica, Nigeria, Ireland and other parts of the world. He is also the Associate Senior Minister of Life Centre Church in Lambeth, UK. His life's mission has been to train and develop individuals to serve local communities, cities, and the whole nation.

As a strong leader who has worked with people all around the world, led hundreds of initiatives and trainings, and brought the message of Christ to people on the streets, Les's unique approach to success has sustained him throughout his many years in leadership.

This one thing he attributes to his success is humility. He calls this concept *servant leadership*

When I asked Les for his definition of success, he said that he will not consider himself to be truly successful until he enters heaven and hears the Father say, "Well done, my good and faithful servant." Every great leader would do well to adopt this attitude of humility. While many people are called to serve as leaders in the kingdom of God, too many of us choose to follow our own aspirations rather than commit to God's calling on our lives. God does not desire our abilities—rather, it is the combination of *God's* ability and our *availability* that brings true success into our lives. Still, any success we experience here on earth will be nothing compared to what Christ has laid up for us in heaven.

And it is this attitude that I believe has propelled many leaders, such as Les Isaac, into fulfilling God's call through unique missions. With this in mind, let's take a closer look at some of the struggles that an attitude of humility can present, and how to overcome these struggles.

BECOMING SOMEBODY

Growing up in the 1960s, Les moved from his home in Jamaica to Britain with his parents. The move was not only difficult for Les because of obvious struggles—like making new friends, going to a new school, and adjusting to a very different culture—but also because it introduced Les to some unexpected personal challenges as well. These challenges revolved around the culture and mindsets that plagued the people around him.

In Jamaica, Les was raised to believe that he was somebody and that he should aspire to do great things. In Jamaica he was taught to do his best to acquire skills. If a young Jamaican was not academically inclined, they were still encouraged to pursue other careers such as construction or marketing. The expectations were higher for young people in Jamaica than they were in Britain, and this change in culture was a setback Les had to overcome.

At school in Britain, Les was exposed to negative and petty attitudes, street gangs, and drugs. To this day, Les is concerned about the urban culture that poisons young people, both in the streets of Britain and all around the world. Les is right to be concerned about this environment: schoolchildren are dealing drugs, both children and teenagers are being shot in the streets, and parents are mourning the loss of their children, whether their deaths be physical or psychological. Les described young people's struggle on the streets as a "fight for survival." He said that Bob Marley's song *Buffalo Soldier* was the perfect articulation of how he felt and how many young people are feeling today. As the song says, they are "fighting on arrival, fighting for survival."

Les was also exposed to social and racial prejudices while growing up, many of which took him many painful years to overcome. Unlike the encouragement he had received in Jamaica, Les was now surrounded by people who told him that he would never become anyone special. They told him to settle for an average life by working at a supermarket. They told him he would never achieve anything great.

Fortunately, today everything has changed for Les. Now, he is the head of many organisations that fight against violence, crime and drug activity on the same streets where he grew up. In spite of these challenges, Les told me that many young people today need someone to give them hope, to tell them that they can make a difference. And, this is the exact message that Les is working to deliver to them.

So when did Les achieve this fundamental change in mentality? And what stopped him from going down the same road as many of his peers? The change came when he found Christ.

In Christ, Les explained, there is always hope. Where there is life there is hope, and it was that hope in a better future and a bigger calling that inspired Les to become a leader. When Les became a believer and was exposed to a different environment inside the church, he encountered the transformational message of the Gospel. Within that message—the same message that he now shares in his church and around the world—Les found grace, righteousness, hope, integrity, and the strength to change.

As he began to grow in Christ, Les quickly discovered that the Bible is a powerful tool that can empower us and change the way we think about every part of our lives. One scripture from which he particularly gained strength was Philippians 4:13:

> *I can do all this through him who gives me strength.*

—NIV

When circumstances got challenging and his journey presented obstacles, Les learned to stay on track by trusting God's process—and, of course, by walking in humility.

During the leader's journey, Les shared, we must all go through a process. We will often face rejection, discouragement, and frustration as we pursue our callings and find our unique purpose. But it is this difficult process that makes us who we are.

Les found encouragement in the truth that all believers have dignity and purpose in Christ. We are called to stand out in the crowd and make a difference. As he fulfilled his calling as a child of God and a fantastic leader, Les found that walking in humility is what makes all those things possible.

ACHIEVEMENT

True achievement has nothing to do with class, colour or upbringing, Les told me: God can call anyone to leadership. Once they begin to grow in their faith and find their mission, however, every leader will discover a variety of very real obstacles.

Les had great leadership abilities as a child, even before he came to Christ. In his school days, Les would lead a crowd of around 200 students or more in destructive drug and gang activity. Although he used his gifts to promote the wrong messages before he became a believer, his leadership ability was still very evident. As I mentioned before, God is looking for people that are available to lead with His purposes in mind. In his teens, Les had been blessed with the skill to lead, but his availability to lead for Christ did not come until he found a bigger purpose.

Les's journey into leadership began when his natural "driver" was turned toward a spiritual purpose: the desire to share Christ with his city and nation. A driver is an internal motivation that determines what we do. We *all* have drivers. Some people's drivers are things like relationships or money, Les said. But after he came to Christ, Les's only driver was to be a great servant leader. That became his motivation, and it is still what drives him to share the message of the Gospel around the world today.

FINDING MENTORS

During our leadership journeys, nothing can accelerate our growth more than finding and learning from great mentors. Through the years, Les has been blessed to find many mentors who have provided him with encouragement and guidance. His mentors have pushed him to do more and be more than what he could ever have imagined on his own.

In your own journey, you may find that others enable you to fulfil God's calling in ways beyond your individual vision. Before he became a leader in the church, Les had a group of church friends that told him he was called to leadership. They had seen his gifts, and told him he was someone that God could use to do great things. These same friends would set up meetings and facilitate opportunities for Les to share his story with audiences—and that was the beginning of his journey as a leader. This is why it is so important to find mentors and learn from them.

John Bunyan wrote of a similar journey in his book, *The Pilgrim's Progress*, nearly five centuries ago. This book is a favourite for Les because its protagonist, Christian, meets different people who show him which way to go and what to do. If it were not for those mentors along the way, who knows how Christian's journey may have ended? It is the same for us today.

Les told me that it is how you finish your journey, not how you start, that matters the most. But he also strongly encourages leaders to seek out mentors, in order to help them grow. How do we find these mentors? Where do they come from?

In the same way that Christian ran into the right people on his journey in *The Pilgrim's Progress*, so too will we find the mentors we need if we're following God's lead and pursuing his mission for our lives. The key is to get started. Some helpful ways to connect with great mentors may include:

☦ Taking them out to lunch

☦ Offering to help with their projects

☦ Buying their books

☦ Attending their events

☦ Listening to their podcasts

Remember that there are many kinds of mentors: some are close friends who you know well, and some are leaders in their fields. All of these relationships can help us on our way to leadership.

Lastly, Les shared that God is not looking for activity, but receptivity: He is looking for people who will remain humble and receptive to his guidance. That leads us to the last key Les shared with me about leadership and humility: prayer.

PRAYER

Prayer is a powerful tool. Although it does many things, one of the most important things about prayer is that it connects us to God. For leaders, connecting with God and hearing from Him on a regular basis is essential.

Being a leader is a great responsibility. We all will face daunting obstacles, and the strength to not give up in the face of adversity and even persecution often requires resilience and determination. It is through prayer that we find the strength to overcome these challenges.

Each morning, Les wakes up around five o' clock and prays. He uses this time to listen and learn what Christ is leading him to do—in his life, in his business, and in the day he is about to face. So no matter what, do not neglect the regular practice of prayer. It will keep you grounded in your identity as a leader, and will equip you to lead with humility.

To recap, here are the keys we have covered in this chapter:

✝ Always walk in humility

✝ Become a servant of Christ and trust Him to make you a leader

✝ Make God's purposes your purposes

✝ Find great mentors

✝ Be available to answer God's calling

✝ Pray regularly

Chapter 23

DELEGATE OR DIE

If they're confident in their purpose and attitude, how can leaders mea-sure their success? Speaking with a brilliant man named Steve Botham taught me that a leader's success is only as great as *success of his team.*

In a business, church, or any organisation, one of the most effective ways to build a great team is to learn to let go of your individual goals. Obviously, this sounds like the exact opposite of what many leaders think they should be doing. However, Steve believes that a fear of letting go reveals that we are more concerned with our comfort level than the growth of our team—which is, of course, what we should be concerned with the most.

"Some leaders think they're cool because they're in control," Steve told me. But in reality, this is a sign of failed leadership. In fact, if we study Jesus's leadership practices, we see that He taught the disciples by pre-senting them with challenges and maximising their abilities. He taught them to lead others and think for themselves. He asked questions. He taught the disciples to solve problems together, without looking to Him for every answer and solution. This is an invaluable example of effective leadership. In light of this revelation, Steve shared with me a manage-ment strategy that he calls the "management triangle."

THE MANAGEMENT TRIANGLE

By using the "management triangle," Steve advises leaders to resolve situations with their teams. In order to create a fruitful environment, he recommends asking the three "A" questions:

✟ First, the whole team needs to experience Awareness. This is the bottom of the triangle and the most fundamental element of the strategy: it means that the team is encouraged to inquire about the situation at hand ask questions of each other and pay attention to any situations that need to be resolved. Good leaders ask their teams "Is everyone on the same page" before the project even begins.

✟ The next element of the strategy is Acceptance. This simply means that the team accepts what has happened or is going to happen. Ask your team: "Does everyone understand the situation?" and make sure there aren't any lingering objections or misunderstandings.

✟ Lastly, the team must take Action. A good leader will encourage their team to ask the right questions at this point, like "What do we do now?" or "What is my role in this project?"

Those three steps form a complete management triangle that Steve has used to teach many teams around the world about letting go and growing together. The point of this management method is to create an efficient environment and a team that knows how solve problems and create solutions—whether or not the leader is always present. As I mentioned earlier, good leadership does not mean that our first priority is to be *in control*. In fact, Steve views true leadership as a process of empowering others.

In the same way that Christ is in the people business—after all, He's all about saving and redeeming people —we should also put people first. Great leaders like Steve always focus on *empowerment*. Jesus was always concerned with enabling his disciples to do more, be more, and think more, even after He left them.

As leaders, Steve explained, we should consistently evaluate how effectively we're empowering others. Every day, we should ask ourselves questions like:

✟ How many people have I empowered today?

✟ Who have I given confidence today?

✟ Have I led with love and compassion? And so on.

This is how Christ led his followers: He empowered, and then He let go. Christ leads with the development of His followers in mind. When He sent His disciples out on their own, he didn't send them out blind and unprepared. Rather, he empowered them to do their jobs well, so that by the time he sent them out they were ready to fulfil their calling. Every leader's journey will look and feel different, but one secret that will apply to us all is a Christlike attitude toward leadership.

Over the years, Steve has counselled and assisted many top business leaders by teaching them how to build better teams. Steve is an executive consultant for Caret Consulting Group in Birmingham, UK, and his strong faith in the church has led him to a position as director of the World Prayer Centre in the Birmingham area and other parts of Europe. While he has learned many key ingredients that contribute to great leadership, he is convinced that learning to let go in order for team growth to be achieved is absolutely vital. So, if you're aiming to lead your team and grow your company, don't hold the reigns too tightly. When you do, you may find that the only thing standing in the way of your growth is *you*.

Besides the Management Triangle, another key concept was shared by Pastor Steve Uppal. Steve Uppal has been Senior Leader at All Nations Christian Centre, Wolverhampton, since 2001. Steve shared with me a few more key concepts that will help you build a strong, dynamic team that I've expanded on for you here. It's important to always stay involved with the day-to-day function of your team. These strategies will enable you to monitor your team's progress as completely as possible, and help you know when you need to step in to help:

PRINCIPLE #1: *CLARIFY THE PURPOSE*

The absolute first step to forming an effective team is to make sure that everyone is on the same page. If you want your team's everyday operations to run smoothly and efficiently, everyone must be familiar with your expectations. Before you even think about introducing your team to a new project, make some decisions about it on your own.

Essentially, you need to have a clear idea of what final result you want from your team. So sit down and do your best to write out a one- or two-sentence summary of the team's mission. This is an excellent opportunity to figure out exactly what your expectations are for the people in your team. Even the most complex projects, in ministry or in business, can be expressed in a concise statement of purpose. Just ask yourself: what is the most essential element of this project? What do you most need to accomplish? What is the most important thing that needs to be done?

Write all of this down now, so that you can refer back to it if the team gets off track later. And, as always, be sure to share this mission statement with your team so that they know where their priorities should lie.

PRINCIPLE #2: *KNOW YOUR TEAM'S GIFTS*

A good leader should always be aware of the gifts that each team member possesses. Hopefully, you're already familiar with all your team members' unique skills and talents simply from interacting with them and observing which work they do well. However, oftentimes people have gifts that you might not know about—or ones that they themselves aren't aware of! Being proactive about getting to know your team might reveal a wealth of untapped talent.

What are some of the practical ways you can achieve this awareness? First, you must get to know your team members on a personal level. Ask them questions like:

✟ Are there types of work that you really enjoy?

✟ What do you see as your greatest workplace strengths?

✟ What role do you see yourself playing in this organisation?

Really take the time to listen to their answers, and evaluate whether their talents and callings are being put to good use with the tasks you are asking them to complete. Perhaps you have someone on your team whose skill set and interests centre on a different area than the one in which they're currently serving. It might be a good idea to move that person to a position where they are in a better position to do their best work.

Of course, not everyone can do exactly what they want to do all of the time. For that reason, you will sometimes need to ask team members to do things which they enjoy or at which they particularly excel. But maximising your team's productivity means trying your best to place people in situations where they will thrive.

Remember: no one knows your team better than you!

PRINCIPLE #3: ORGANISE THE TEAM

Once you've familiarised yourself with your team members' gifts and potential, you are in a great position to decide which positions are best suited to which people. This gives you an edge when trying to determine the best, most efficient organisational structure.

Before you give your team a new job, break the project down into the specific roles and tasks that need to be completed. Then brainstorm whose talents and skill sets could be best applied to each of those roles. Think of this stage of the process as drawing up a blueprint that your team can refer back to during their day-to-day work. You want to clearly articulate how the team should work when you aren't able to be around.

After you have made these decisions, your leadership role is really just beginning. In order for your decisions to be effective, you must clearly communicate how you envision the team's structure. Nothing hampers a group's effectiveness more thoroughly than confusion about which people are supposed to be serving which roles. So sit down with your team and explain who will be in charge of which tasks. Designate some members to supervise different aspects of the project, and make sure those people are equipped with the tools they need to succeed. Make sure that everyone understands who they will be working with, who they will be reporting to—whether it's directly to you, or to another supervisor—and which tasks you expect them to complete before the job is done.

Solicit questions and concerns from everyone, and find out if there are any parts of the plan that people are having a hard time understanding. It's much easier to sort through potential misunderstandings early in the work process than to waste valuable time fixing mistakes later. Many errors can be avoided through this simple practice. Always remember that teams in which each person understands their place in the structure will function in a smooth, orderly fashion.

PRINCIPLE #4: COMMUNICATE THE SCHEDULE

The most important projects have some sort of timetable or deadline. It is crucial for the group to understand the schedule that you're expecting them to operate with, so make sure that you don't forget this important piece of information when you're outlining your expectations. Does the project need to be completely finished in a week?

Uncertainty about these factors is one of the biggest reasons why organisations operate at less than optimum productivity, and the stress from a surprise deadline can put massive amounts of pressure on everyone involved. Incompetent leaders often fail to give their teams a complete picture of the schedule from which they are working, which can frequently lead to mistakes, miscommunications, and—most importantly—missed deadlines.

The bottom line is this: if your team doesn't know what you expect from them, they will not know what to expect from each other. So give them as much information as you can about the timetable, as well as any important deadlines that might be on the table. Your team will thank you!

PRINCIPLE #5: *SUPERVISE THE PROCESS*

If there is one telltale sign of a bad leader, it's someone who drops an important assignment on their team, only to disappear from the picture until the deadline. There is nothing more frustrating, from a group member's perspective, than a leader who does not take an active interest in the team's success.

In contrast, a great leader always involves themselves with their team's work. They consistently check in to see how the process is going and are totally familiar with any problems or successes that have arisen along the way.

Of course, there are practical ways that you can stay aware of the team's progress. The best way to do this is to stay in constant communication with the team's leaders. Meet regularly with the people who are working in supervisory roles. Understand any concerns that they might have about the expectations that you have set.

This will help you figure out when you need to intervene or offer some guidance to the team. Ideally, the guidelines that you've set out before beginning a project will enable the team to function smoothly in your absence, but this is certainly no reason not to be consistently involved with your team. The more thorough your planning has been at the beginning of the process, the less likely it is that you will need to offer guidance in its later stages.

Hopefully these strategies have given you an easy-to-understand blueprint of how to build successful, dynamic teams. To review, here are the keys we have covered in this chapter:

✝ Teach your team to be effective—even when you're not around

✝ Use the management triangle (Awareness, Acceptance, Action) to solve problems

✝ Envision your team's end goal

✝ Clearly communicate your schedule and expectations

✝ Be involved with every step of the process

✝ Lead with compassion, love, and clarity

✝ Be willing to let go of control of your team

✝ Follow Christ's example and focus on empowering people

In the previous chapters of this book, we have gone over many details about leadership based on lessons from some of the top leaders around the world. We have covered topics like vision, team growth, church plant-ing, fund-raising, listening to God, and fostering your team's productivity and growth. We have learned that effective leadership does not mean doing everything on our own, and we have learned that being a great leader is more than just holding a head title in an organisation or busi-ness. Now, as a final lesson on productivity and leadership, I will share with you some strategies to be a more effective leader in administration.

Time-management is by far one of the most valuable skills you will ever develop. Before we dig deeper into this essential key to leadership, understand that time management does not always mean multi-tasking, working yourself to the bone, or never having time to rest or play. On the contrary, managing time is more about learning to organise your priori-ties. One of your greatest assets in accomplishing this feat is having a great team behind you.

At age 42, Dr. David Carr suffered from a major heart attack. Although he made a full physical recovery, David's personality changed drastically after the event: he learned to ask for help. As a successful businessman with many years of experience in the financial and marketing industries, his workload was as full as it could be without killing him. He was working six days a week, managing books for clients in the National Football League, and trying to spend time with his wife and three children, all at the same time. On top of all this, he traveled frequently, and had visions and dreams he wanted to accomplish. As a believer, David felt that he was called to go into ministry. So he enrolled in classes studying theology for five years.

He took time off from his business duties one day a week to study, but still struggled with his workload. The problem? He was terrible at administration, and had difficulty delegating tasks to other people. Some of us have to learn things the hard way, and I suppose that was the case for my friend David. Being a leader is about knowing which things to delegate to others, which things to pursue ourselves, and which things to let go. Trying to do everything on our own is possibly the best way to kill ourselves—in David's case, literally.

Around the time of his heart attack, David was managing a church that was growing rapidly and in need of a full time pastor. Trying to be a businessman and a pastor at the same time proved to be a struggle that David would have to find answers for—and quick. As it turned out, the solution was better time-management and smarter delegation.

THE EIGHT HOUR FORMULA

Today, Dr. Carr is the Senior Pastor of Renewal Christian Centre in Solihull, UK. He travels the world as a writer, speaker and pastor, sharing his message all around the globe. His life has been an amazing chronicle of overcoming obstacles, and he consistently spends his time helping others and doing great things for the kingdom of God. None of this would be possible, however, if he had not learned the art of administration and time-management all those years ago.

These days, David has a system in place, a formula that he uses to structure each of his days. It's called the eight-hour formula. David looks at his time and his days differently than most people: he sees his time the way successful leaders do, as his most valuable resource.

We all have 24 hours in a day, right? So the key to successful time-management is to make the most of every hour in every day. To do this, David breaks up his days into 3 sections: mornings, afternoons, and evenings. Each section represents 8-hour blocks of time.

To get the most out of your day, you have to do some math and first determine what David calls your *non-negotiables.* Non-negotiables may include the hours you have to spend in the office, the hours you need to sleep at night, or anything that you simply must do every single day. Estimate your non-negotiables as accurately as you can; for example, some of us need less sleep than others. Once you have found these non-negotiables, write them down and add up how many hours in your day you have left. For instance, if you sleep seven hours each night that would leave you with 17 hours left in your day. This concept is fairly simple, but the application can be tricky—especially when the list of things we "have" to get done never seems to end.

This is when we must evaluate our priorities. For David, that meant making enough money to pay the bills, while endeavouring to pastor a church and run a business all at the same time.

How is this possible, you may ask? It's simple, really: it's all about priorities. Sorting out your priorities is the key to good time-management.

Realise that everything on your list of daily tasks may not be a real priority. Some things may not be as important as you think, while the important things may be in the incorrect order. By organising your priorities, you are setting yourself up for true success.

Before being forced to maximise his time, David was working six full days a week selling pensions—and he could still barely pay the bills! Fortunately, he learned the power of up-selling. By moving into selling corporate pensions, as opposed to regular ones, David found a way to pay all the bills by only selling one pension a month, leaving him more time to focus on his ministerial calling. Now that's managing your time!

Devote some time to figuring out how to make your day work for you, and how to get the most value out of the least amount of hours. This is the secret to becoming great in business and in life: you need to learn, like David, to see your time as your most valuable possession.

So, what are you doing with your time? How many hours do you have after you subtract the non-negotiables? Are your priorities in the right order? Once you have answered these two questions, you can rearrange your current schedule to match your goals and priorities. Should your mornings be used for sales, emails, or phone calls? Should you use your evenings to make connections with new clients, or arrange meetings? Determine what works best for you. But make sure that none of your precious time is ever wasted.

As Benjamin Franklin said: "Lost time is never found again." Never forget that truth, and be sure to make the most out of the hours you have.

David says that there are four questions that every leader should ask: *Can it? Will it? Could it? Should it?* Once you've answered "yes" to each of these questions, then you can *do it*. Great leaders will ask questions that make the most of their time. If a job isn't really necessary, then it is a waste of time. If an employee is valuable and knows how to do something better than you can do as the visionary or business owner, then trying to do it yourself would be a waste of time. Asking for help is difficult for many leaders, especially at the beginning of their journey, but it is a crucial key to time-management.

GROWING YOUR TEAM

Once you have done all that you can do to maximise your time, the next step is to call in a team of people that will help you leverage your time in ways that you can't do yourself. Think of Jesus: he did some of his greatest miracles after he had enlisted the help of his disciples. We too, must learn to ask for and accept help when it is needed, if we want to become effective leaders.

I mentioned that David was horrible at administration before his over-work began to endanger his health. So how does someone who is horrible at managing others get better? By learning to let go and hand off responsibilities to others. You must be willing to accept feedback, both positive and negative, and you absolutely must ask for help.

David was often frustrated in his early years as a visionary, especially in his ministry. He often found that he had too many ideas to keep up with on his own. After realising he needed help, he started to learn about administration. At first, he wasn't very good at it: he would give unreasonable tasks and set unrealistic deadlines, and was terrible at communicating with his team. But now, after years of working as a successful administrator, he has learned a few lessons along the way. These principles can apply to any organisation, and will be particularly helpful for leaders looking to grow their teams.

LESSON #1: COMMUNICATION

Communication is probably one of the most important things you need to develop as a leader. Clear and specific communication about responsibilities will save time, frustration, and money for everyone involved. By properly communicating your needs, expectations, and tasks, leaders give their teams the tools that they need to be most effective. So give your team early notice about tasks that need to be done and make sure they understand all of the details. Technology may help to lighten the load for those who aren't naturally adept at communicating. As an example, David can always be seen with his handy IPad, which he uses to take notes and draft emails for his team; this extra communication makes sure that the job gets done even when he isn't around to supervise. Use whatever helps you be more efficient in communicating with your team. It's important to leave no gaps unfilled.

LESSON #2: DEADLINES

Before he learned about communication and administration, David would completely blindside his team by announcing projects on to his church members without telling his team beforehand. Then he would give his team a deadline that was completely unreasonable because they had never been prepared. This kind of task management is flawed: it will never get the job done, and it will make the whole team feel out of the loop. They should never feel that way, so make sure that you give your team reasonable deadlines. Don't set them up for failure in the process.

LESSON #3: *APPRECIATION*

Showing appreciation for staff and employees is a crucial element of great leadership. Leaders and visionaries are often so busy seeing the big picture that they can unknowingly come across as ungrateful for our team's hard work and effort.

Behaving with compassion, as a pastor or a businessperson, is always the best policy with the people who are working to make your life easier. Although your team may not always give you exactly the feedback you want to hear, it's full of people who want you to succeed and will always be there to help you. So don't be afraid to ask for help—but always make sure to say thank you in return.

Leaders like David, who understand that you cannot do everything on your own, have learned the secrets to successful leadership that we've outlined in this chapter. And these key differences are only a few of the qualities that separate good leaders from great leaders.

So whether you are called to ministry, business, or both, try applying these strategies of time-management and stewardship. With their help, I believe that you too will quickly build a team of great players that will help launch you into your calling and destiny!

As a quick review, here are the keys we have covered in this chapter:

✞ Don't be afraid to ask others for help

✞ Divide your day into 3 separate sections

✞ Learn to manage your time effectively and make the most of every hour

✝ Find out which tools best help you to communicate, and use them

✝ Set reasonable expectations for your team

✝ Always say thank you

CONGRATULATIONS!

You have just completed the final chapter in **The 5 Core Abilities of Highly Effective Leaders.** In this book, we have learned many timeless lessons from great leaders like Steve Botham, Bil Cornelius, Dr. David Carr, Rabbi Daniel Lapin, Todd Gongwer, Jenni Catron, Marisa Shadrick, Rev. Les Isaac, and Perry Marshall, Kate Coleman and many many other **outstanding Christian leaders.** We've learned that leadership is a huge responsibility, both in the kingdom of God and in the secular marketplace. We have also learned that none of us are born as great leaders, but are each called by God in His own time to fulfil a purpose and bring glory to Him.

Therefore, I want to encourage you to keep leading as Christ leads, and to never give up on God's call for your life. May God bless you in your leadership journey!

To listen to all the interviews with the leaders referenced in this book, go to *www.errollawson.com/podcast*

The 5 Core Abilities Coaching and Mentoring Programmes

In every generation there are leaders that stand above the rest. They are recognised for their contribution and the results that they achieve. Opportunities come looking for them. They are able to attract other high achievers to support their cause. These are the types of leaders we have to develop our teams to be.

For those who want to implement the 5 core abilities method quickly and powerfully we provide one to one and group coaching for leaders and their leadership teams.

We are able to work with clients anywhere in the world. The focus of the program is to enable you to apply the best practices in this book with guidance from world-class mentors, creating a culture of high performance within your organisation.

Our mentoring team include successful entrepreneurs, established church leaders, celebrated leaders and world-class experts.

To find out more, contact us today to book a discovery session by emailing admin@errollawson.com.

Download the brochure and take the challenge at
www.the5coreabilities.com